HOPE AND HISTORY

JOSEF PIEPER

HOPE AND HISTORY

Five Salzburg Lectures

Translated by Dr. David Kipp

IGNATIUS PRESS   SAN FRANCISCO

Title of the German original:
Hoffnung und Geschichte:
Fünf Salzburger Vorlesungen
© 1967 Kösel-Verlag GmbH & Co., Munich

The text of this book reflects—in only slightly altered form—the manuscripts of lectures presented by the author at the "Salzburger Hochschulwochen" in August 1966.

The epigraph by Pascal is the concluding part of a sentence from the *Pensées* that reads as follows: "Le présent n'est jamais notre but. Le passé et le présent sont nos moyens; le seul avenir est notre objet" (*Œuvres de Blaise Pascal*, vol. 13, ed. by Léon Brunschvicg [Paris, 1921], 89f., [no. 172]).

Cover by Roxanne Mei Lum

© 1994 Ignatius Press, San Francisco
ISBN 0-89870-465-0
Library of Congress catalogue number 93-78535
Printed in the United States of America

QUI

MAGNI AD CONVIVII SPEM

ALACRIUS NOS PRÆCURRIT

DILECTO FILIO

PIAM IN MEMORIAM

CONTENTS

I

"For the first time": the new urgency of the question (13); "The deceived wiser than the never deceived" (14); Kant: "What may I hope?" (17) Interpretation of linguistic usage (19); The "precipitous good" that lies outside our control (23); The one object of hope per se (25); "Fundamental hope" and "everyday hopes" (26); Disappointment as enabling hope per se (28); Only he who hopes anticipates nothing (31)

II

Historical and nonhistorical events (33); Freedom and decision (34); The hope of martyrs (35); Teilhard de Chardin and the confusion of evolution and history (36); A test case: evil (40); The temptation to resignation vis-à-vis history (46); Not a "jungle" but a mystery (46); The limits of speculation (47); The historical future and prophecy (47)

III

The arguments of the idealistic philosophy of progress (Kant) (53); Questionable visions of the future (58); Futile use of names of traditional concepts and loss of overall meaning structure (60); The "angle" of evolutionism (Konrad Lorenz) (62); "God has entrusted the world to their decisions" (64); Teilhard de Chardin on the final state of the earth: two mutually exclusive hypothetical models (65); "Strike in the intellectual-spiritual sphere" and "ecstasy of discord" (68); The collapse of evolutionist thought and the admirable aspect of Teilhard de Chardin (70)

IV

Ernst Bloch and his encyclopedia of images of hope (75); What is nevertheless missing? (76); Misunderstanding about God's other-worldliness (77); Realization of hope through "socialist transformation of the world"? (79); *Ubi Lenin, ibi Jerusalem!* (81); The ignoring of death (84); Expectation of a golden age as "consolation in the hereafter" (86); The unanswerable question of legitimization ("How do you know that?") (90); Success of the "plans" worse than their failure? (93)

VI

Faith's challenge to revealed prophecy about history (95); Eschatology and apocalyptics (98); Everything becomes false if the believed total conception is wrong (99); No continuous progress up to fulfillment (100); "Passing from time into eternity" (Kant) (101); Not simply the "victory of reason" (103); "The lie made into the world order" (Kafka) (104); The last word of apocalyptic prophecy: New Heaven, New Earth (106); The Great Banquet and the *spes implicita* (109); The non-specifiability of the object of hope (111)

Index   115

"We seek the city that is to come."

Hebrews 13:14

"The future alone is our objective."

Pascal

I

In the last decade of the eighteenth century, that is, the decade of the French Revolution, someone both raised and attempted to answer the question of whether the human race is constantly progressing toward the better. This someone was Immanuel Kant.[1] His discussion of the matter takes a very fundamental approach —nothing has been decided in advance, or at least so it seems. Considered quite abstractly, he says, there are obviously three possible answers to the question: (1) "constant ascent", (2) "continual decline", and (3) persistence at a given level, advancement on a more or less unvarying plane. Of these three possible answers, Kant finds that one can be immediately excluded, from the very start and without any discussion, namely, the second. "Regression to the worse" (as he expresses it) is, to be sure, an abstract possibility; but *in concreto*, there is no such thing; it is simply inconceivable to

---

[1] Due to withholding of permission to publish (in Berlin), the relevant treatise, although written in 1792, did not appear until 1798 (in Halle); Kant incorporated it into his work "Der Streit der Fakultäten" (*Gesammelte Schriften* [Ausgabe der Preuß. Akademie der Wissenschaften], vol. 7 [Berlin, 1917], 79ff.).

Kant. Why? The explanation provided here reads literally as follows: "Decline toward the worse cannot be an ongoing constant in the human race, for at a certain stage in that process it would wipe itself out." But this possibility, the self-destruction of the human race, is—according to Kant—totally out of the question in the context of realistic thought about history; such a thing can never happen.

Now, in the meantime (although, to be sure, only in the most recent past), a radical change has clearly occurred in relation to this point; fifty, or even just thirty, years ago, people could rightly believe themselves to share this conviction of Immanuel Kant's. After Hiroshima, one can no longer do so. Since then, the idea that humanity could "wipe itself out" not only has become thinkable or merely discussable but is also of immediate urgency.

Looking back at this position of Immanuel Kant's, one is reminded of Kierkegaard's bitter maxim that the man who has been deceived is wiser than the one who has not. Also, one may perhaps find it unfair to argue about this matter, from the superior vantage point of the "deceived", with a man of the eighteenth century, accusing Kant, for instance, of a deficiency of understanding or methodological exactitude. For at that time, the self-extermination of man was in fact beyond the realm of concrete possibility; it was, from a purely technical standpoint, something not realizable. Within the framework of his historical presuppositions, was Kant not, then, actually right? I would say that he had his good reasons but that he was not right. After all, the nature of historical man has not changed since then, indeed, not even since Adam (or Cain)! About the possibilities, including that of destruction, that are inherent in historical man; about what he can be deemed capable of—about this it was undoubtedly easier for Kant to make a mistake than for us today; but it remains a mistake nonetheless, an error. Today, we are probably more susceptible to other sorts of error about man, but at least we are immune to this Kantian one. Confronting the three possible forms of the course of history that were formulated by Kant, we would be simply incapable of excluding the one—the negative one—from the very start.

This is confirmed in countless ways by the cultural-critical, historical, philosophical, and sociological writings of recent decades as well as whenever an attempt is made to define the special position of this present age of ours. "Today for the first time the existence of man is threatened, *for the first time*"—thus begins an address delivered at an international symposium of scholars in London (in 1962) on the future of man,[2] a future that the participants otherwise all tend to assess too optimistically. And of course the fact attracting most attention is precisely that technical possibility—impossible to discuss away—of man's self-destruction through his own, self-manufactured weaponry. Robert

[2] *Man and His Future*. A Ciba Foundation Volume, ed. Gordon Wolstenholme (London, 1963), 315.

Oppenheimer says, "Never before has the world had to face up, as it does today, to the possibility of being destroyed, indeed, absolutely annihilated; never before to a decision as difficult as that about the cessation or the continuance of the world."[3] Another well-founded historical-philosophical diagnosis is summed up in the following sentence: "We are the first men to have control of the apocalypse."[4] It is, of course, a most questionable turn of phrase to speak of men having "control of the apocalypse"; but the intended meaning, I think, is fully clear. In any case, it suggests yet again that no one pondering the historical future of man can simply leave out of account the possibility of catastrophe. Moreover, the situation of the questioning itself becomes maximally acute inasmuch as the questioner and ponderer can no longer indulge in the self-deception of presuming to enjoy, so to speak, a state of "academic" detachment—as if there were no end of time available for first thinking the problem through in a fundamental way and then discussing whatever solutions might suggest themselves. *These are not long-term problems*—this observation was made repeatedly at the London symposium;[5] what concerns us here are not problems reaching far into the future. "A long life", Konrad Lorenz says, can hardly be prophesied for man if one observes without prejudice "how he stands there

[3] *Drei Krisen der Physiker* (Olten and Freiburg im Breisgau, 1966), 81.

[4] Günther Anders, *Die Antiquiertheit des Menschen* (Munich, 1961), 242.

[5] *Man and His Future*, 363.

today, holding in his hand the hydrogen bomb that was the gift of his reason, and in his heart the . . . aggressive drive that the just-mentioned reason is incapable of mastering". This sentence can be found, by the way, in a book bearing the title *The Hopes of Our Age*.[6]

So here we encounter, with almost provocative effect, the first of the two basic terms that are conceptually linked in the subject of these lectures on "hope and history". No matter what concrete implications might happen to follow from the question thus formulated, it is at least clear from the start that the mere linkage of these two concepts is of unparalleled relevance in our present-day situation. Here, too, we could speak of unprecedentedness—*for the first time*; never before, it seems, has it been possible to ask the question about the meaning and justification of human hope with such acute urgency. And yet, just what question, precisely, is at issue? That cannot, of course, be answered without first clarifying to some extent how "hope" and "history" are to be understood here.

~

What, then, is "hope"? As we know, Ernst Bloch's great book *Das Prinzip Hoffnung* (The principle of

[6] *Die Hoffnungen unserer Zeit. Zehn Beiträge* (Munich, 1963), 147f. The ideas expressed in Konrad Lorenz' contribution, "Die Hoffnung auf Einsicht in das Wirken der Natur", recur almost to the letter in his book *Das sogenannte Böse. Zur Naturgeschichte der Aggression* (Vienna, 1963).

hope)[7] begins with the challenging thesis that "in previous philosophy" the subject of hope has hardly been addressed at all; hope is "not included in the history of the sciences"; it remains "unexplored like the Antarctic"; and he, Ernst Bloch, intends to "bring philosophy" to this undiscovered land. In this connection, one might nevertheless make the point that Immanuel Kant[8] had already considered, as one of the four basic questions to which he says "the field of philosophy" can "be reduced", that of "What may I hope?" He immediately adds, however, that this question is answered by religion! There is, incidentally, a touch of irony in the fact that precisely this grounds an objection raised against Ernst Bloch from the side of orthodox Marxism (which he himself claims, at the same time, to represent). The condemnatory verdict passed by the party critics in Leipzig on Ernst Bloch's work can be summed up in one sentence: "The philosophy of hope is religion",[9] and in Marxism there is no "place for any sort of religious problem".[10] It looks, in fact, as if the concept of hope, inasmuch as it unavoidably brings to expression the religious dimension, must necessarily become a controversial one. Even the area of historical

[7] Frankfurt am Mainz, 1959, 4f.

[8] *Gesammelte Schriften*, vol. 9 (Berlin and Leipzig, 1923), 25.

[9] Manfred Buhr, "Kritische Bemerkungen zu Ernst Blochs Hauptwerk *Das Prinzip Hoffnung*", *Deutsche Zeitschrift für Philosophie* 8 (1960): 366.

[10] Manfred Buhr, "Der religiöse Ursprung und Charakter der Hoffnungsphilosophie Ernst Blochs", *Deutsche Zeitschrift für Philosophie* 6 (1958): 590.

interpretation cannot, so it seems, remain untouched by this fundamental controversialism; for instance, the Protestant theologian Conzelmann maintains that the entire "family of words related to 'hope' in Greek antiquity lacked any religious connotation"[11]—which is demonstrably false, I would say, without looking beyond the example of Plato.[12] But the point need not be pursued here.

In any case, hope is something that can be empirically encountered and understood; this seemingly undeniable function of the human psyche presents itself continually to our experience. Consequently, those who reflect upon existence as a whole, that is, those who philosophize, cannot avoid focusing on hope as a phenomenon and discussing it—doing so, of course, in a philosophical way, which means from every conceivable viewpoint.

Once again, then: What is hope? What do people mean when they speak of hope and hoping? Our initial aim here must be to draw out their meaning on the basis of man's living, spoken language. Incidentally—as will be seen later—such an elucidation of linguistic usage is by no means an easy task, and the results can be quite surprising. But first and foremost,

[11] "Hoffnung", in *Religion in Geschichte und Gegenwart*, vol. 3, 3d ed., col. 417.
[12] For example, the expression "highest hopes" in Aristophanes' speech in the *Symposium* (193d) derives from the language of the mystery cults; cf. Gerhard Krüger, *Einsicht und Leidenschaft*, 2d ed. (Frankfurt am Mainz, 1948), 315.

by what other means could one expect to arrive at a reasonably binding definition? Who else is to determine what is to be understood by "hope"? Arbitrary definitions are of little use to us, no matter how precise they may at first seem to be—like, for instance, this famous definition from Spinoza's *Ethica*: "Nothing other than an inconstant pleasure arising from the image of something regarding whose outcome we are in doubt"![13] Does this say anything at all about the decisive essence of hope? Plain common sense, at any rate, will fail to recognize its conception of hope in this definition—which, for example, fails to mention the element of expectation that living linguistic usage seems to regard as an essential aspect of hope. Of course, I can also expect something without being at all able to say that I was hoping for it; something unimportant or even terrible can also be "expected". But I speak of "hope" only when what I am expecting is, in my view, *good*. The concept of "good" is to be understood very broadly here ("good weather"; "good that you have come"), signifying, in its original sense, all that one longs for.[14] Longing, yearning, desiring, wishing, hungering, and thirsting must all play a role in it; otherwise we do not speak of hope. However, I can also long for something and wish to have it while at the same time knowing that I will never get it—something, therefore, that I can hardly be "hoping" for. Hope, by

[13] Pars III; propos. 18; schol. 2.

[14] Aristotle, *Nichomachean Ethics*, I, i, 1094 a 3; Thomas Aquinas, *Summa theologica*, I, 5, i.

contrast, includes an element of confidence; it is inconceivable apart from even a kind of certainty, although one difficult to define precisely. Yet there is, to be sure, also a hoping in vain; there are hopes that are disappointed and ultimately shattered. That the one who hopes, however, while and as long as he hopes, could be certain of this futility—that is something beyond imagination; the impossible, something thought to be impossible or even recognized as impossible, is never hoped for. In such a case, nobody uses the word "hope".

What one hopes for is something welcome, desirable, loved: something good that can really be granted to him. This links up with the fact that there is no hoping without an element of joy. Perhaps we cannot say that joy enters directly, as a conceptual component, into the definition of hope; but it is nevertheless something that constantly accompanies hope —because hope is aimed at being granted something good and thus something loved, while joy is by nature nothing other than the response to being granted what we love.[15] Hence, the opening descriptive phrase given in Hoffmeister's dictionary of philosophy,[16] according to which hope is "joyful expectation", goes right to the heart of the matter.

---

[15] Cf. Josef Pieper, *Glück und Kontemplation*, 3d ed. (Munich, 1962), 43ff.
[16] Johannes Hoffmeister, *Wörterbuch der philosophischen Begriffe*, 2d ed. (Hamburg, 1955), 304.

Yet all this still falls far short of conveying the whole of what the notion of hope really means: in the sense, it should be remembered, of the living speech of ordinary people. In that context, it is quite possible that one might be expecting, with joy and confidence, something both wished for and longed for, yet nobody would call such expectation "hope"; one would simply not use that word. For example, echoing Joseph von Eichendorff, someone might utter, in the most heartfelt way: "Come, this world's comforter, thou silent night"—but does one "hope" for the arrival of night? Nobody would say such a thing. One does not "hope" for something that occurs anyway and necessarily, and particularly not for something that one is convinced will necessarily come about—a fact that, by the way, is rather rich in potential consequences. For instance, anyone who regards classless society as something that will come about through rigorous natural laws would therefore also be implying that it cannot, strictly speaking, be an object of human hope. But discussing this further here would be premature, since we are still concerned with drawing out the constituent aspects of the concept of "hope" as understood in everyday, living language.

Now, not only do we refrain from speaking of hope in relation to something that will happen with certainty anyway, as well, but in that which can be gained easily and, so to speak, "without cost". I might well "hope" to gain something at no cost and without personal effort, but I would speak like that only when getting something at no cost is precisely not just an assured prospect! The ancients spoke of the *bonum arduum*;[17] only a good that is "laborious"—i.e., something hoped for that is not already just there for the taking, something that could, although I am not actually in doubt, nevertheless remain denied to me.

Along with this, we catch sight of another constituent aspect of the concept of "hope". The thing hoped for, in the strict sense, is beyond the control of the one who hopes. Nobody says that he is "hoping" for something that he can produce or obtain himself. In order to grasp this fact, one need only consider, in a random way, examples from actual linguistic usage: "I hope that we'll have good weather tomorrow"; "I hope that the train will come on time"; "Let's hope that we all stay healthy". People hope that there might never be another world war; they hope for a good harvest, for the prosperity of their children, for a long life, and so on. What is common to all these everyday expressions is quite clear: what is hoped for is always something over which the one who hopes has no real power—perhaps he can do a little to help things along, but regarding what is decisive he is powerless; he cannot simply cause, generate, manufacture, produce, or create the thing hoped for. Were that not the case, then no sensible person would speak of hope. When an artist begins the task of translating his creative concept into a material work of stone, or perhaps

[17] Thomas Aquinas, *Summa theologica* I–II, 40, 8.

of verse, and when he says that he hopes he will meet with success, he thus gives fully appropriate expression to the fact that this success does not depend on him alone. And when a craftsman speaks to me of his hope that he will be able to meet the delivery date for the desk I have ordered, he then lets me know, again fully appropriately, that he is dependent upon various circumstances and other persons that are not within his control. Were that same craftsman to assure me, however, after we had discussed the nature of the project in precise detail, that he confidently hoped the desk would turn out as agreed in our discussion—then, of course, I would justifiably become doubtful and begin to wonder whether it might not be better to engage someone else for the job, since nobody uses the word "hope" in relation to something that he himself is really capable of doing! A concerned father might well appeal to the conscience of his high-school student son by saying, "I hope you will work harder from now on"; but if his offspring were to respond that he hoped so, too, then that would be nothing but impertinent nonsense. All of which, taken together, implies something both very serious and highly momentous; Gabriel Marcel[18] formulated it as follows: "The only genuine hope is one directed toward something that does not depend on us."

~

---

[18] *Position et approches concrètes du mystère ontologique* (Paris, 1949), 73.

24

But language—the language that is not only spoken by everyone but also directly understood and on the basis of which something becomes clear to us as truth inasmuch as we recognize it as something we had "always" known—language, I say, holds in store for us still other pieces of information that we would at first hardly suspect. In Plato's *Symposium*,[19] Diotima speaks of the peculiar fact of linguistic usage that, although there are many people who "make" something and many kinds of "things made", there is nevertheless only one who is designated a "maker" per se, namely, the *poietés*, the poet. Similarly, there are also many forms of love: love of country, love of parents, love of friends, and so on; and yet, when one speaks simply and without further qualification of "lovers", what are meant are not those who love their country or their parents, but only lovers in the erotic sense. A similar peculiarity, it seems to me, can be found in the area of linguistic usage centered on hope. Thousands of different things, from fine holiday weather to world peace, can be objects of human hope and are, in fact, such objects. Yet, once again, there appears to be only one single object that, by being hoped for, renders a person simply "one who hopes". Probably the situation here will be more clearly evident if expressed in the mode of negation. There are thousands of hopes that a person can give up and lose without thereby becoming purely and simply "hopeless"; it is apparently only one kind of hope, the hope

---

[19] *Symposium*, 205 b–d.

for one sort of thing, whose loss would mean that he had absolutely no more hope and would be purely and simply "without hope". The question is just what the object of this one hope might be. What is the thing that a person would have to have abandoned or rejected hoping for if we are to be justified in saying of him that he had lost hope per se, that he was now absolutely, wholly, and utterly without hope?

This, I believe, is a question that cannot be adequately answered or even discussed if one has not first taken account of a certain distinction for which precisely corresponding terms are apparently lacking in the English and German languages. In French, however, there are two different words for "hope", namely, *espoir* and *espérance*, whose distinctness—which is difficult to grasp—consists partly in the fact that each has a different relation to plurality: *espoir* tends toward the plural, toward the "thousands of things" that one can hope for, whereas *espérance* seems rather to exclude plurality. Indeed, Paul Ludwig Landsberg (in his unfortunately almost forgotten little book *Die Erfahrung des Todes* [The experience of death])[20] had suggested that, in the interest of clearer representation of the actual situation, one should draw a distinction between "hopes" and "hope".

The significance and fruitfulness of this distinction first really came to light, however, through the results of some research undertaken in recent years in

[20] Lucerne, 1937, 48.

the field of medical anthropology. Here I refer mainly to the phenomenological analyses of the Heidelberg internist Herbert Plügge,[21] who conducted extensive clinical studies of the inner state of certain people for whom, in a unique way, hope had become a problem—of the inner state, namely, of the incurably ill and of persons who had made an attempt to take their own lives. Proceeding at first purely empirically, this approach also found itself confronted with a two-part structure of hope: along with commonly so-called hopes in particular, there emerged unexpectedly "another hope"[22] (one almost senses the surprise of discovery in Plügge's account of this). This "other" hope Plügge terms "fundamental", or also "authentic", hope —as distinct from the "ordinary" or "everyday" hopes (in the plural) that are directed toward something "in the worldly future", toward an "object belonging to the world", toward something presumed to come to us from the outside, whether it be a communication, a success, a useful commodity, or even a restoration of health. "Fundamental" hope, by contrast, appears to have no object that can be found to exist in the world in this "objectlike" way. There is, then, nothing specific and concrete that can be pointed to; it is directed toward something "indefinite", "nebulous",

[21] Herbert Plügge, *Wohlbefinden und Mißbefinden. Beiträge zu einer medizinische Anthropologie* (Tübingen, 1962). For present purposes, two of the essays are especially significant: "Über suizidale Kranke" and "Über die Hoffnung".
[22] Ibid., 44.

27

"formless", "unnameable"—for which reason fundamental hope is much more difficult to characterize in any way.[23] Gabriel Marcel—regarding this (as he says) "absolute sense of 'I hope' ", which he (also!) explicitly distinguishes[24] from "I hope that"—speaks almost as if this "absolute" hope had no object at all; in any case, it tends to transcend all "particular objects" and cannot really be grasped until one stops trying to imagine the thing hoped for.[25] But of course there is certainly "*something* hoped for", even if its mode of being is quite different from that of all objective goods and all conceivable changes in the external world. In the context of interpreting his medical case histories, Plügge says that fundamental hope (singular) is not directed toward anything that one could "have" but rather has something to do with what one "is", with one's own being as man; what is hoped for in it he provisionally describes as "self-realization in the future" and as "well-being of the person".[26]

∼

The aspect of Plügge's findings that is really worth thinking about, if also likely to surprise at first, seems to me to be his observation that true hope does not emerge and show its face until the moment when

[23] Ibid., 44 ff.
[24] *Homo viator* (Paris, 1944), 43.
[25] Ibid., 43, 60.
[26] *Wohlbefinden*, 44 f.

one's various "hopes" are finally disappointed, fall to pieces, and lose their meaning—only then can "fundamental hope . . . most convincingly be grasped"; this is actually an opportunity offered by disappointment for the "purging of all illusory hope"; "out of the loss of ordinary, everyday hope arises authentic hope".[27]

"Disappointment" is thus to be taken (in the literal sense of the German word *Enttäuschung*) as a "disillusioning" that frees from illusion (or deception). The illusion, the perhaps at first totally unavoidable self-deception, consists in our believing that the attainment of certain goods in the objective world, including bodily health, constitutes existential well-being or is at least necessary to it. Disappointment, by contrast, suddenly puts us in the position of experiencing and "realizing" something that we had perhaps already suspected, namely, that real well-being consists not in some other thing alone but also involves ourselves as hoping for (and having always hoped for) this "other" from the very depths of our soul, with a much more vital, a truly unconquerable, intensity. Hence, "disappointment" implies far more here than the correction of an erroneous belief; it implies liberation in a sense extending far beyond the realm of the cognitive. Plügge says that the experience of certain knowledge that one is incurable possibly provides the basis for a freedom from captivity to one's illness

[27] Ibid.

that "could not have been gained prior to that final collapse".[28]

There are many reasons to assume that this finding is valid beyond the specific situation initially focused on here, i.e., that of the incurably ill; ultimately, in relation to a "fatal end", we are all, without exception, in the same situation. Every deep disappointment of some hope whose object was to be found in the worldly sphere potentially harbors an opportunity for hope per se to turn, without resignation and for the first time, toward its true object and, in a process of liberation, for existence to expand, for the first time ever, into an atmosphere of wider dimensions. Precisely in disappointment, and perhaps in it alone, we are offered the challenge of entering into this broader existential realm of hope per se.

~

There is no necessity, of course, to take up this challenge. Nobody *must* hope. One can also refuse to do so; one can lose fundamental hope and reject it. Nevertheless, it cannot, strictly considered, be disappointed; rather, it is exactly as unshakable, for its part, as existence itself.[29] Disappointment rests on a kind of experience; it comes about because some hope has been shattered, has shown itself to be vain, has failed to fulfill itself. But precisely this experience of nonfulfill-

[28] Ibid., 45.
[29] Marcel, *Homo viator*, 62.

ment is virtually impossible in relation to fundamental existential hope.[30] Why is that? Because the point in time at which the true result of one's life becomes evident remains something still to come for as long as that life itself persists! At no specific moment of existence —not even at the threshold of death—can a person say, "I am now no longer moving forward; fulfillment no longer lies in the future." One who despairs, who rejects fundamental hope and is thus simply "without hope" (even if, "closer to the surface" as it were, hoping for thousands of things, which nonetheless remains of no ultimate significance), is therefore, strictly considered, not someone who has been disappointed. He has by no means experienced nonfulfillment; rather, he anticipates it. Despair is the anticipation of nonfulfillment.[31] There is also, of course, the anticipation of fulfillment, but that is equally at odds with the reality of our existence as wayfarers (*viatores*).

The one who hopes, and he alone, anticipates nothing; he holds himself open for an as yet unrealized, future fulfillment while at the same time remaining aware that he knows as little about its scope as about its time of arrival.

∿

[30] This is not to deny, of course, that despair can possibly be claimed to rest on experience; it is just that the experience cannot be one of existential hope's being positively disappointed.

[31] Cf. Josef Pieper, *On Hope* (San Francisco, 1986), 51, 70.

If, as this initial circle of thought comes to a close, we turn once again to the formulation "hope and history", one of the questions it raises would apparently have to be this: Is the nature of human hope such that it can be at all satisfied within the realm of history? Nothing of any importance can be said about that, however, until it is clear just what is to be understood by "history".

II

The German word for "history" (*Geschichte*) derives, as is generally known, from the word for "happening" (*Geschehen*). But not everything that happens, it would seem, is history; there are also nonhistorical events. A lightning strike, a landslide, the flow of rivers, the sea tides—such things are always "happening", yet they are not historical events in the strict sense. Seemingly a bit closer to the properly "historical" are the sprouting, growing, blossoming, and fruit bearing of a plant; and closer still, an animal's being born, growing up, pursuing its prey, and then perhaps itself falling prey to a more powerful predator. Whenever we speak of a process of "becoming", we can also speak, with some justification, of "history". It is not at odds with linguistic usage to describe the "origin of the species", the emergence of life, or even the genesis of the universe itself in terms of "natural history" or the "history of the cosmos". In all of the foregoing, however, the word "history" still seems to lack the specific sense that makes a process the potential subject of a historian, of the actual "writing of history". It has been asserted that an event, including perhaps even a lightning flash, becomes "historical" in the precise sense of the word through that event's having "some relation to men".[1] Yet not everything that happens to us, or even everything that we do, is for that very reason history. Birth, maturation, aging, dying—these physiological and factual processes are not, strictly considered, our "history". And even the things that befall us in an objective sense during our lifetime—gaining or losing possessions, health, or attractiveness; being endowed with innate qualities of intelligence, temperament, or constitution; the fact that certain people cross our path: a teacher, an adversary, someone beloved—these incidents and encounters are likewise not, in themselves and because they occurred, our history. The really crucial thing is what we ourselves make of all this! Both kinds of factor combine to determine the full nature of what actually comes to pass. It is an intertwining, then, of what destiny presents to us and the personal response that we ourselves contribute to this that first gives rise to genuine "human history" as well as to "history" per se in the full, proper, and exact sense of the word. Hence, an event becomes historical when what is specifically human comes into play in it: freedom, responsibility, decision, and therefore also the possibility of willful blunder and guilt. In contrast, precisely this accounts, first, for the essential singularity, the unrepeatability, and the noninterchangeabil-

[1] Walter Brugger, *Philosophisches Wörterbuch* (Freiburg im Breisgau, 1947), 122.

34

ity of the truly historical, but above all for the fact that a historical event is by no means predictable or deducible from things that have already occurred.

~

At this point, something should be said about the difference between history and evolution, especially since present-day discussions seem to show increasing signs that this eminently important distinction is in danger of becoming obscured.

On one occasion, it appears, at a lecture given in Paris in 1951, I was honored to have Pierre Teilhard de Chardin present in my audience. Not until ten years later, unfortunately, after that man had died, did I learn of this fact; at the same time, however, I also learned that he had passionately rejected the position I was arguing. My topic was "The Hope of Martyrs" (*L'Espérance des Martyrs*); the lecture was presented during the *Semaine des Intellectuels*, which was held under the motto "*Espoir humain et espérance chrétienne*".[2] My purpose was to make clear that it is not worth talking seriously of hope if there is no hope for martyrs, that is, for persons whose expectations in this world, indeed, whose prospects of mere survival in the struggle for realization of justice, have been wholly and utterly annihilated and who therefore find themselves, to all appearances, in an absolutely despairing situation: in jail

[2] *Espoir humain et espérance chrétienne. Semaine des Intellectuels Catholiques* [May 24–31, 1951] (Paris, 1951), 76–84.

awaiting execution, in a concentration camp, stripped of all rights, mocked, abandoned, exposed to the scorn of the privileged. It is, by the way—as Erik Peterson has pointed out[3]—nowhere written that the martyr, from a Christian viewpoint, has to be a comfortingly exceptional figure, cropping up only every now and then in extraordinarily hostile circumstances; and I did not, in my lecture, leave this fact unmentioned. But my central thesis, as I have said, was this: it is better that we remain silent about hope if there is none for the martyr.

Now, this is what Teilhard's spirited opposition was directed against—this defeatist way of framing the question in the first place, this, as he puts it, "Christianity of flight". According to him, the main question, which has priority over all else, was not even mentioned, namely, whether "man, objectively considered, beyond all sentimentality, philosophy, and mysticism, but viewed bio-cosmically [*biocosmiquement*], is justified in having hope. Regarding man, are we concerned, in a purely empirical sense [*expérimentalement*], *hic et nunc*, with a child, with a youth, with an adult —or perhaps with an old man? In other words, just what, in the year 1951, from an evolutionary viewpoint, is man's likely potential? To my dying breath, I will shout the following into all deaf ears of pseudo-existentialism and pseudo-Christianity: this alone is the question [*toute la question est là*]." Those were the com-

[3] "Zeuge der Wahrheit", in *Theologische Traktate* (Munich, 1951), 200.

36

ments of Teilhard de Chardin (in a letter published by his biographer, Claude Cuénot).[4] What he is claiming here, then, amounts to this: considered with a view to its evolutionary potential, mankind is still objectively young and therefore full of energy for the future—and thus we have grounds for hope.

Now, this is precisely what I would call a confusing of history and evolution! Although the situation here is, of course, somewhat complicated, devoting a moment to it would be well worthwhile; in hardly any other context, it seems to me, can the decisively historical be grasped as clearly as when it is contrasted with the concept of evolution.

There is obviously nothing to object to in the claim that man must not be considered apart from the evolution—stretching over millions of years—of the cosmos as a whole. Rather, man occupies an irreplaceable position within that evolution; according to all that we know, he could not have appeared on earth any earlier or any later than he actually did. Possibly a case can also be made for assuming that the evolutionary process did not come to a halt after arriving at man. In any event, one can justifiably refer to man as an "evolutionary phenomenon"; he is, as Teilhard says, "first and foremost a cosmic phenomenon" (*un phénomène cosmique . . . d'abord*).[5] Furthermore, processes like development, the unfolding of what is already present but

[4] Claude Cuénot, *Pierre Teilhard de Chardin. Les grandes étapes de son évolution* (Paris, 1958), 316.

[5] In a letter published by Cuénot (ibid., 428).

undeveloped, or evolution are certainly also found in the specifically human; spiritual life itself takes place to a large extent as evolution. In prehistoric man's very first reach toward the forces of nature, in the earliest ways of utilizing some form of energy in the material world, such as fire or water power—in those very beginnings something was present but undeveloped that then began "unfolding" itself, with logical consistency and almost "over his head", all the way to the point of providing access to atomic energy! And there is not the slightest reason to doubt that man will continue developing and perfecting, to an unforeseeable degree, all his achievements in this field. Regarding this opportunity for progress, one can feel quite reassured and look to the future with full confidence.

Here, admittedly, I begin to falter—inasmuch as there are, in fact, sufficient reasons for not being confident at all, regarding, for example, the perfecting of atomic weapons. Here something new comes into play, something that cannot simply be grasped in concepts associated with the notion of evolution. Our discomfort does not have its cause in any doubts about the evolutionary potential of technological intelligence; no trace of doubt exists there. What disturbs us is something quite different, namely, worry about just how man, as a creature whose decisions are made in freedom and responsibility, will treat the immense power that has become accessible to him and what he will actually use it for.

But these observations, it seems to me, make the difference between evolution and history palpably plain. In Teilhard de Chardin's main work on the phenomenon of man,[6] there is a sentence that brings the two aspects together: "If mankind makes use of the enormous span of time still available to it, then it has immense possibilities before it." The potential of the *énorme durée* and the *possibilités immenses* (mankind is still young!)—that, of course, is the aspect of *evolution*. But the "if", the uncertainty about whether the possibilities are actually likely to be used and realized—that is the aspect of *history*. What really happens, and what will happen in the future, is decided, however, not on the plane of evolution but on the plane of history. And it is only what really happens that affects us directly; it alone touches our existence. The question about the biological-genetic potential of humanity does not deprive us of any sleep, but the question about our historical future quite likely may. "The Future of Man" —this is the title of an essay by the American evolutionary scholar Hermann J. Muller,[7] who was awarded a Nobel Prize for his work in the field of human genetics; this essay, which describes "man's future conquests over outer and inner nature", also concludes with that word "if": "Thus we see the future for man as one of his own making, if only he will have it so."[8] But if man does not have the will, then everything will happen

[6] *Le Phénomène humain* (Paris, 1955), 317.

[7] "The Future of Man", in *The Humanist Frame*, ed. Julian Huxley (London, 1961), 409.

[8] Ibid., 414.

differently. This happening differently, and also, incidentally, the conscious directing of evolutionary forces through the planning of men—all this is obviously no longer just evolution but rather history.

~

Regarding history, however, the validity of that optimism can no longer be taken for granted that, if not a conceptual component of the idea of evolution, nevertheless quite naturally accompanies it—"naturally" because evolution *eo ipso* implies ascendance, development, progress. Thus it appears to me simply fallacious to say: take a look at evolution up to the stage of man, at how unerringly it has pursued its course—and you will then be assured that, regarding human history as well, there can be no catastrophic end. It should not be left unnoted that it is Teilhard de Chardin who asserts something of this sort.[9] The argument, however, simply does not hold up; its consolatory thrust fails to affect us. Once again, the fundamental distinction that separates evolution and history has been ignored.

Part of the essence of history is that it rests upon freedom and decision—and that it can therefore be marked by the presence of evil, whereas any use of that concept in relation to evolution would naturally be pointless. In that sense, Konrad Lorenz' wording of the title of his book on *so-called* evil was quite right,

[9] *Phénomène,* 306.

although he of course meant this differently. Freedom, however, is not solely, and not primarily, freedom for evil and destruction, as has been claimed, for instance, by someone like Immanuel Kant. "The history of nature begins with the good, for it is the work of God; the history of freedom, with evil, for it is the work of man"—this sentence is from his essay entitled "Mutmaßlicher Anfang der Menschengeschichte" (Presumed beginning of human history).[10] As just indicated, I consider the equating of "freedom—work of man—guilt" to be an inadmissible oversimplification, that is, to be false. Nonetheless, it is this "history of freedom" that at least contains in itself the possibility of guilt; and it is only this "work of man" that we call "history" in the strict sense. Therefore, the problem of evil, of negation, of guilt serves as something like a criterion and a test for determining whether the decisive attribute of the phenomenon of "history" has become at all evident or not.

Were one to call political tyranny an "occasional hypertrophy"[11] (along with things like the fluffy hats worn by British Guardsmen or the "wasp-waist" look in female fashion), then the critical question is not whether this might not imply an inordinate downplaying of the problem of evil in history but rather whether the phenomenon of evil had been perceived and identified at all. Teilhard de Chardin, in a brief summing

---

[10] *Gesammelte Schriften*, vol. 8, p. 115.
[11] Bernhard Rensch, *Homo sapiens* (Göttingen, 1959), 112.

up of his general theoretical position (as of 1948),[12] attempted to interpret the existence of evil as a "statistical necessity" (*nécessité statistique*), i.e., whenever a large number of individual creatures is in the process of organizing itself into a unity, anomalies will necessarily occur with a certain frequency—which he illustrates with what might be called a "postal" example (in the process of masses of letters being sent by mail, certain errors regularly occur, like incorrect postage, incomplete addresses, etc.). Once again, it must be asked whether such an interpretation—which, admittedly, follows quite logically from the standpoint of evolutionist thinking and is perhaps unavoidable—in any way captures the phenomenon in question here? I would say no!

This is not to deny the existence of comprehensive general laws that are partly determinative of the fully individual actions of men and therefore also render them statistically quantifiable. Rather, what I am venturing to claim is this: in the midst of the evolution of the cosmos, which also shapes the nature of man's being; in the midst of "natural history", which includes that of mankind; alongside and outside of the many other sorts of "development" (more or less predeterminable as regards direction and pace) of intellectual life, in the sciences as in the arts, in the technological mastery of natural forces—apart from all that

[12] "La pensée du Père Teilhard de Chardin, par lui-même", *Les Études Philosophiques* [Paris] 10, no. 4 (1955).

42

and in the midst of it (this is my thesis), there is also a fully different, irreducible, incomparable, and in the strict sense "historical" kind of event that issues from the free decisions of men, comes about through them, and itself participates in the mode of being proper to human acts of will; which means, for instance, that it cannot be predicted or calculated on the basis of evolutionary or historical laws and above all that it possesses, beyond any mere factuality, the quality of having to be "answered for" and of being "good" or "evil".

∼

Anyone, however, who reflects on this extremely complicated interplay of things—who makes only a mere attempt to interpret this interactive process, which is conditioned in an incomprehensibly many-sided way, extending from merely natural occurrences up through many intermediate levels and beyond to free human action; who scrutinizes these dynamics, laden, so it seems, with all too many variables and unknowns in order to gain deeper insight into the structure of the whole or even just a more exact notion of what actually takes place—such a one may be tempted simply to give up and to declare as patently unanswerable not only the question of whether there is a final, comprehensive "meaning" to history but even the question of how to determine what happens, "in truth", in the here and now. One should not, it seems to me, find such temptation all too surprising; on the contrary, it would be more surprising if analyzing the chemical composition of some active organic substance, or answering some other question in the area of natural science, were to be less difficult than achieving a definitive conception of man or of some phenomenon from the sphere of human existence—that *has* to be incomparably more difficult! In America, I once heard the magnificent aphorism that understanding the atom is child's play compared with understanding child's play.

Strangely enough, by the way, it is not empirically minded historians but rather theologians who insist most uncompromisingly that cognizance of the true face of the historical process, of events that take place before our own eyes, is not possible for us. "What truly happens . . . cannot be discerned within history itself";[13] "history conceals, in principle, its meaning; it plays itself out as a mystery";[14] it cannot "itself enjoy" its own "eternal content";[15] "the history of the world is not itself the judgment of the world";[16] history is "present only as a fragment", and that fragment "can be completed by nobody";[17] and "we cannot know which of the forces of history ultimately subserves the

[13] Heinrich Schlier, *Die Zeit der Kirche* (Freiburg im Breisgau, 1956), 265.

[14] Ibid.

[15] Karl Rahner, *Schriften zur Theologie*, vol. 5 (Einsiedeln, Zurich, Cologne, 1962), 121.

[16] Ibid., 120.

[17] Hans Urs von Balthasar, *Das Ganze im Fragment* (Einsiedeln, 1963), 13.

Kingdom".[18] These quotations all come from modern theologians: Heinrich Schlier, Karl Rahner, Hans Urs von Balthasar, and Yves Congar. Altogether, they make a protest against any claim to be able to capture the meaning of history or the true significance of particular events in some convenient formula—whether that formula be theological, evolutionary, or sociological in nature and whether it be based on an idealistic or a materialistic interpretation of historical laws. Yet none of these authors seems to hold the opinion that history is something obscure in itself, something confused, a "jungle". Use of the term "jungle" can be found in modern sociology; one of its representatives[19] states that anyone seeking an ultimately valid orientation to the course of history can "unfortunately" no longer avail himself of the "trick used in previous sociology"; such a one is "today no longer" able to position himself "on some mountain, or even some hill, of insight"; rather, it becomes clear to him, precisely in pondering the question concerned, that he finds himself "in the midst of the jungle". This kind of self-denial is, I believe, in fact the only fitting response that is possible from the standpoint of a sociologist; the mountain or hill of insight was never, even previously, something that he could legitimately ascend. Even present-day theology does not claim, when con-

[18] Yves Congar, *Der Laie. Entwurf einer Theologie des Laientums* (Stuttgart, 1957), 158.
[19] Helmut Schelsky, "Zur Standortsbestimmung der Gegenwart", in *Wo stehen wir heute?* ed. H. W. Bähr (Gütersloh, 1960), 196.

sidering the phenomenon of history, itself to be situated on such a mountain.

Nonetheless, the quotations just cited are not simply an expression of resignation. They are obviously open to attack from two directions. On the one hand, as already noted, they oppose the possibility of deriving from the course of history anything like a basic structural formula whose application would then render everything explicable, regarding not merely the past but also the future (and it is, after all, not just a purely imaginary assumption that theories making precisely that sort of claim could arise in philosophy of history!). On the other hand, this theological thesis is directed against the despairing absurdism of the nihilistic variety of existentialism, which asserts the absolute meaninglessness of the historical process and walls men up within their concrete factual circumstances, within the "jungle" of an accidental and arbitrary situational dynamics. Theology does, of course, speak of the mystery of history, but a mystery is not a "jungle". And the other basic notions mentioned, like "judgment of the world", "eternal content", or "Kingdom", signify the opposite of resignation.

Inasmuch as theology expands the scope of empirically accessible history into a realm of trans-empirical reality; or more precisely, inasmuch as it testifies to the conviction that the history we can experience derives its meaning, which we cannot immediately experience, from being anchored in a more comprehensive, universal structure in which the concepts of "eternity",

46

"Kingdom", and "judgment of the world" have their place—inasmuch, I say, as theology points the vision of the person immediately caught up in concrete historical events beyond the realm of the empirical, it thereby gives him the opportunity of understanding, in that situation, that he does not know what, here and now, is truly happening.

The fundamentally important thing about this theological conception—which thus admittedly does nothing to overcome the indecipherability of the concretely historical—seems to me, initially, to be simply its factual presence. I find it clearly remarkable that such ideas have been worked out in a serious way and that an intellectual structure like this should even "exist". The real significance of it all, however, does not come to light until the question about the historical *future* has been posed. For that remains indecipherable in a special way; precisely in relation to the strand of the "historical" in the strict sense, the future resists any kind of advance calculation or speculation.

～

Here, once again, the gap between history and evolution shows itself. Someone who knows the "evolutionary potential" of a given situation may very well be capable of predicting a future development. And perhaps it is really possible to establish, with adequate precision, whether humanity as a species, "viewed biocosmically", *biocosmiquement*, is still young. But in what way could one possibly manage to ascertain whether humanity, even if perhaps still "young", will annihilate itself or not? Here freedom and choice are in play; here, to phrase it differently, we have to do with the "historical" in the precise sense of the word—assuming that one would not want to resort to understanding the self-extermination of man (initiated, perhaps, with the help of access to atomic energy) as an organic-developmental defect and interpreting it, on the model of the extinction of certain prehistoric animal species, as a result, for example, of "the excessive enlargement of some organ, in this case, the cerebral cortex" (an idea that, while seeming completely absurd to me, is actually advocated by an important German evolutionary scientist).

At any rate, in relation to the strictly "historical" future, every method of advance calculation proves inadequate—no matter how much (with the aid, for instance, of computers) the procedures of statistical forecasting may be perfected. Any sensible forecaster knows that quite well. Wilhelm Fucks, whose much-discussed *Formeln zur Macht* (Formulas for power)[20] have often enough been misunderstood, says, for example, with a view to his own theses, that "all calculations" would "come to nothing" were a world war to break out and be conducted with the weapons available today. I myself once offered the following hypothetical example for consideration. On the basis of statistics, it

[20] Fifth ed. (Stuttgart, 1965), 158.

could undoubtedly have been predicted, several years in advance and with a high degree of exactitude, how many fatal traffic accidents would occur in April 1945 in the city of Danzig. But that the city of Danzig itself would scarcely be still in existence at this time, that there would, in any case, be no traffic there at all—that could not have been known in advance and certainly not on the basis of statistics.[21] In the *Pensées* of Pascal, there is an aphorism well worth considering in this context, although it seems at first fairly impenetrable; one can understand it only by taking into account the year of its authorship. The aphorism reads, "Would a man who enjoyed the friendship of the King of England, the King of Poland, and the Queen of Sweden ever have thought that he would find no place of refuge in all the world?"[22] The year of authorship was 1656. In that same year, the Polish King, John II Casimir, was dethroned; two years before that, Queen Christina of Sweden, then twenty-eight years old, had made a free decision to abdicate; and as for the King of England, Charles I, not yet seven years had passed since his execution under Oliver Cromwell. Hence, there was no longer any place of refuge in the world for anyone who had been relying on his friendship with them, as improbable as that will have seemed! No biological or historical laws could have led anyone to suppose something like this, and even the best-informed

[21] Josef Pieper, *Über das Ende der Zeit*, 2d ed. (Munich, 1953), 38f.
[22] Aphorism no. 177, in the numbering of the edition by Léon Brunschvicg; *Œuvres de Blaise Pascal*, vol. 13, p. 93.

observer of political affairs would have been incapable of foreseeing these events—because all three of them had their origins in the decisions of men, or, to put it differently, because they were "historical" events in the strictest sense of the word. An event that is really historical, that is concrete in every respect (e.g., about the who, when, and where, which alone interests those actually affected)—the historical as understood in this way simply cannot be grasped through speculation.

It is implicit in the concept of prognosis that the probability of something in the future is inferred on the basis of certain "clues" in the past, especially in that most recent past that we call the "present". The skill of the prognosticator consists precisely in discovering and interpreting, within the already available store of facts, within the history that has already been realized, certain signs that indicate, though hidden to the average mind, what is to come. And if, *post festum*, the prognosticator "lays his cards on the table", he will be able to show exactly what formed the basis for his inference that things would happen as they did. However, since an event that is historical in the strict sense is precisely one that cannot be inferred from the existing store of facts; since free, spontaneous decision is, *per definitionem*, in play, so that even what is most probable need not happen while what is most improbable can happen —for that reason, once again, the historical can never be reached through speculation. And if the historical future were able to be grasped at all, then it could be only through a form of foretelling that would have to differ from prognostication by having no need of proceeding on the basis of past facts. With that, I have almost formulated a definition: the definition of *prophecy*.

The question, then, is whether there is such a thing as credible and, in this special sense, "prophetic" insight into the historical future of man. If there is no such thing, then no justifiable statement can be made about how human history will progress and even less about how it will end.

III

Attempts have often been made to achieve a depiction of the future of historical man *without* having any recourse to prophetic intelligence.

Kant, for example, expressly lays claim to being "able to predict, without any reliance on prophetic vision",[1] humanity's continual progress toward the better. Teilhard de Chardin, too, proposes to speak of the possible "final state of the earth" purely "on the basis of cold logic", *froidement et logiquement*, and "without any element of apocalypse".[2] And obviously the *docta spes* spoken of by Ernst Bloch is not informed by the teachings of the prophetic books of Holy Scripture but presents itself rather as "hope understood in a dialectical-materialistic sense".[3]

A certain representative status can, incidentally, be attributed to those three authors; and it is no more than fitting and proper to take thoughtful account of the conceptions of the future put forward both in the idealist philosophy of progress and in evolutionist

[1] *Gesammelte Schriften*, vol. 7, p. 88.

[2] *Phénomène*, 305.

[3] *Prinzip Hoffnung*, 8.

cosmology, as well as in a quite distinctive, mystical-eschatological version of Marxism—although, to be sure, it will soon become evident that none of these provisional descriptions is precisely appropriate.

~

What separates *Immanuel Kant*, for instance, from problem-free believers in the religion of progress is, on the one hand, precisely his being disturbed by the opposing arguments: whether "eternal peace" might not really be just a pleasant dream of philosophers;[4] whether events might not, grotesquely enough, take such a course that man would "improve himself to death";[5] or whether "out of wood as crooked as that of which man is made" it is likely that anything "quite straight" could be constructed.[6] On the other hand, all of this tends to lend his own position an increased compellingness and weight—even though not, of course, making it any more accurate. Nor is it exactly made any plainer by the fact that Kant takes up concepts and images clearly derived from the Christian religious tradition but then goes on to use them in a completely untheological sense. Thus, for example, he speaks of the "kingdom of God on earth" as the "final destiny of man", yet what he understands by "kingdom of God" is most peculiar. When, namely, the supplanting of the Faith of the Church by the religion of reason has

[4] *Gesammelte Schriften*, vol. 8, p. 343.

[5] Ibid., vol. 7, p. 93.

[6] Ibid., vol. 8, p. 23.

won public, state-based recognition and sanction any-where in the world (a thought obviously formulated with an eye to the France of the revolutionary years; Kant wrote this in 1792)—then one could "say with reason that the kingdom of God had come to us".[7] This interpretation, unworthy of discussion and alien-ating as it is (one would want to ask whether a concept intended to keep the sphere of human thought open is not being misused here precisely for the purpose of too hastily closing it) nevertheless does not, I be-lieve, imply an outright rejection of the prephilosoph-ical, the sacred tradition; rather, a very characteristic kind of intellectual conflict is manifest here: an effort, despite a fundamental commitment to rationalism, to keep the trans-rational dimension of historical existence at least within visible range. This sort of thing can be found more than rarely in Kant's work. For example, in discussing the "education of the human race as a whole" (in his late, anthropological lectures),[8] he says that man can expect this to come "only from provi-dence, i.e., from a wisdom that is not his own but is nevertheless the impotent (due to his own guilt) idea of his own reason"—and such a sentence contains, I be-lieve, more than a little theological content. And Kant seems to be prevented often enough by (as called by Thomas Mann)[9] "being ashamed of God" from using

[7] Ibid., vol. 6, p. 122.

[8] Ibid., vol. 7, p. 328.

[9] *Briefe 1937–1947* (Frankfurt am Mainz, 1963), 305. Cf. also 15 and 410.

55

(for example) the term "providence" when that is definitely what, at bottom, he means. Thus he finds, for instance, that the term "nature" is "more in keeping with
the limitations of human reason . . . and more mod-
est than the expression . . . 'providence', which implies insolently assuming Icarus-like wings in order to
draw nearer to the mystery of its unfathomable intention"[10]—whereby, once again, he is doubtlessly much
closer to the spirit of Christian theology of history
than, for example, is Hegel, who (expressly making a
polemical point against Kant) maintains unreservedly
that "the key to world history" is "given" to us[11]
and that Christianity possesses "a definite knowledge
of providence and its plan".[12]

It was necessary to say a little about these compli-
cating aspects of the Kantian conception in order to
avoid an overshallow understanding of his doctrine on
progress, which, after all, had a determining influence
on his ideas about the historical future and the end
of history. At any rate, when he brings himself to
the point of giving a straight answer, with no beat-
ing around the bush ("What do we want to know
here?"),[13] he responds to the question of "whether
the human race is continually progressing toward the
better" with a clear yes. But how does he justify that

[10] *Gesammelte Schriften*, vol. 8, p. 362.

[11] G. W. F. Hegel, *Vorlesungen über die Philosophie der Weltgeschichte*,
ed. G. Lasson, vol. 1 (Leipzig, 1930), 22f.

[12] Ibid., 23.

[13] *Gesammelte Schriften*, vol. 7, p. 79.

yes? He is convinced that it can be justified in no way
other than through experience. It would therefore have
to be possible to discover some "event" within empirical history that points to the presence of a progressive
force in humanity, and indeed, so compellingly that
one would necessarily have "to infer, as its inevitable
consequence, the reality of progress toward the better."[14] Kant is of the opinion that such an event can,
in fact, be identified.

Initially, one might suppose that the reference here
is, once again, to the French Revolution. It is, however,
not the Revolution itself but rather, as Kant puts it,
the "sympathetic response", almost "approaching enthusiasm", that the Revolution evokes "in the hearts
of all onlookers".[15] But just why, one asks himself,
is this supposed to fulfill the criteria applicable to the
kind of "event" being sought here? Kant gives the following answer. This sympathetic response "evidences
. . . (because of its generality) a quality characteristic
of the human race as a whole and, at the same time
(because of its unselfishness) a moral quality, at least in
dispositional form, . . . which not only justifies hope
for progress toward the better but is itself already such
progress". So far so good, but how does the argument
continue? It does not, in fact, continue at all! Un-
believably, Kant regards the argument as having been
concluded with what he has said. At most, one could
add that he characterizes the above-mentioned "sympa-

[14] Ibid., 84.
[15] Ibid., 85.

thetic response" more precisely by identifying its object: it pertains to the desire for a kind of state that cannot be "addicted to war", namely, for a republican one. But the argument itself is at an end. Concisely formulated, it amounts to this: in one representative instance, humanity as a whole has decided in favor of what is morally right; hence, things are getting better for it. Nothing remains but to state the conclusion formally: "As regards the human race, then, I claim to be able to predict, without any reliance on prophetic vision, its advancement, in a no longer wholly reversible way, toward the better".[16]

It is almost inconceivable that this critical thinker, who has both staked out and restricted the boundaries of human knowledge, can go on to say that this is by no means just well-intentioned talk aimed at soothing men; no, "despite all unbelievers", it is a "proposition tenable even in the most rigorous theoretical context that the human race has always been advancing toward the better and will continue to do so".[17]

But perhaps what Kant has in mind here is advancement in relation to certain sublime moral qualities that are not at all perceptibly represented in what we commonly call "history". No, he means concrete, political history; future progress will show itself in that. For example, "Gradually the use of force by the powerful will diminish, while obedience with respect to laws will increase"; above all, people "will find themselves obliged

[16] Ibid., 88.
[17] Ibid.

58

to turn war, first, into something gradually more humane, then something less frequent, and finally, as aggressive attack, something wholly extinct"[18]—and so on. Now, words need not be wasted on the fact that, for those recently living through two world wars, this kind of argument is as good as worthless.

The Kantian conception of the intratemporal "end" of history will also, I fear, not be especially persuasive to us. Things are generally happening, he says at first,[19] in such a way that, "among the advancements of the human race, the cultivation of talents, artifice, and taste" are running ahead of "the development of morality"; but one day, "in time to come", "humanity's moral disposition" will catch up. Concretely translated, this apparently means that, for a period of time, the achievements of civilization, such as mastery over nature, have come about, largely and even quite "naturally", without moral control; more concretely still, it is thus quite natural that, for a period of time, humanity should know how to deal technically with atomic energy without, however, yet being capable of making sensible use of it. Obviously, these extreme possibilities of the mastery of nature could not have entered Kant's field of vision, but they are what really put the force of his argument to the test. Is the span of time available for "catching up" not perhaps too short? *These are not long-term problems.* Kant is confident. But on what grounds?

[18] Ibid., 91, 93.
[19] Ibid., vol. 8, p. 332.

He cites two: first, the "experiential proofs of the moral superiority of our age as compared with all previous ages"[20] (there is clear reference here, once again, to the French Revolution); and second—something mentioned, to be sure, only in passing and parenthetically but nevertheless actually cited—our entitlement "to hope" for such "under the governance of a wise ruler of the world".[21] I could not presume to decide which of these two grounds of proof Kant saw as having the greater force (although I can detect, I think, a slightly ironic tone when he characterizes the first argument, based on "faith in virtue", as "heroic").[22] His conception of the end, too, is sufficiently hedged with qualifications: we should, he says, "probably be able to nourish the hope that the Last Day might dawn more with an ascent like Elijah's than with a . . . descent into hell and bring about the end of all things on earth".[23] It is surprising that Kant describes an end conceived in this way as a "natural" end—expressly to be distinguished from a "supernatural" or an "unnatural" one, of which he also speaks[24] (albeit purely hypothetically, as if speaking of something that, for him, is out of the question).

However, the magnificent thing about the Kantian conception of the historical future consists precisely

[20] Ibid.
[21] Ibid.
[22] Ibid.
[23] Ibid.
[24] Ibid., 333.

in the fact that almost all the elements of grand, traditional eschatology are still somehow present, are at least mentioned by name: time and eternity; kingdom of God and providence; the self-incurred burden of human existence;[25] there is even talk not only of the New Heaven and the New Earth[26] but also (if only *in abstracto*) of the possibility—described, moreover, in the old phraseology as the "reign of the Antichrist"[27] —of a final intra-historical catastrophe. The bad and hopeless thing, of course, consists in the fact that the overall intellectual structure—which alone could enable each of these elements, in itself, to have a meaningful place—has long since lost its organizing force. That Kant felt a foreboding of this seems to me evident precisely in the sense of strain, in the (so to speak) despair of his thinking about history, including its ironical self-relativization. In post-Kantian thought on history, however, that "difficult" intellectual structure continues to disintegrate with an uncanny inner logic—for many reasons, among which must surely be numbered an increased rigidity and sterility of tradition. At any rate, the end result—which cannot be explained in terms of the willfulness of individual thinkers—is likewise unalterable, at the time, by the best intentions of the individual.

In this situation, simply becoming resigned, declaring one's ignorance, and keeping silent appears to be

25 Ibid., 332.
26 Ibid., 327f.
27 Ibid., 339.

the most honest response to the question of just where this whole thing called "human history" is ultimately going—assuming, however, that such silence does not imply the absence of anything at all beyond the empirically knowable, that one could meaningfully ask questions about here. Still, keeping the questions alive in a fully open spirit but nevertheless resisting the temptation to provide a seemingly exact, overhasty, and in the negative sense "conclusive" answer—that, as I said, would seem to me not the worst of responses to the riddle of history, and in any case one incomparably more convincing than whatever might be proposed as possible solutions, or even "the" solution, from some specialist angle.

~

Evolutionary science is also such an angle. Considered as a whole, of course, one can speak of it only with respect and admiration; its findings have quite fundamentally corrected, broadened, and deepened our entire view of the world. And man, too, can no longer be conceived other than as a being having his irreplaceable position in the genesis of the cosmos and deriving his life from the evolutionary impetus of creation as a whole. Here, I admit, the reservation formulated by Adolf Portmann[28] also strikes me as deserving of wholehearted support: one should not believe that evo-

[28] "Probleme der Evolutionstheorie", *Merkur* 14, no. 141 (1960): 850ff.

lution itself is anything like "a process already comprehended in principle".

Above all, however, the evolutionary way of thinking remains, in relation to the topic "history", a necessarily restricted viewpoint from which—as has already been discussed here—the undiminished reality of man acting in history cannot become visible at all. For that reason, any attempt to apply the intellectual apparatus of evolutionary theory to interpreting the historical problems of the present, and even to justifying a "declaration of hope", must arouse extreme mistrust from the very start. "Avowal of hope"—that is the heading of the final chapter in Konrad Lorenz' much-discussed book *Das sogenannte Böse* (On so-called evil [English edition: *On Aggression*]). Once again, one can speak with nothing but admiration of the infinitely rich documentation of experience by the behavioral scientist Konrad Lorenz; often enough, we must catch our breath as his masterly descriptions make us eyewitnesses to his fully original observations. This, however, only serves to heighten our consternation when we then learn not only what the author has to say about the overcoming of our historical threats but also what forms the basis of his hope.

Lorenz sees the situation of contemporary man as being determined primarily by two elements: the factual availability of weapons of nuclear destruction and an "aggressive drive" that is apparently beyond rational control. In this situation, he goes on to say, there is "incontestably" a need for an "inhibitory mechanism" that "blocks violent aggression not only against our personal friends but also against all men".[29] Yet it is, of course, absolutely impossible for us, "the way we are constituted", to fulfill the need for an active love of a kind that extends to all men. This "constitutedness" of ours could, however, very well be altered, not by ourselves, naturally, but by—whom? By evolution! "Evolution can do this";[30] "the great constructors can do this",[31] namely, the "constructors" behind the altering of the species: "mutation" and "selection".[32] And then comes the "avowal of hope": "I believe that they will do it"; "I believe that this will endow our heirs, in the not all too distant future, with the ability to fulfill that greatest and most beautiful requisite of true humanity."[33]

What is apparently being claimed, then, is that the man of our time should, and can, hold the hope that he will be set free (without needing to do anything himself) from the suicidal situation of the atomic age through genetic changes in his physical makeup that can be expected to occur in the course of further development—and will thus, perhaps, turn him into another kind of being! Here one might well prefer to side with the Marxists[34] or with the biblical saying

[29] *Das sogenannte Böse*, 412f.

[30] *Die Hoffnungen unserer Zeit*, 159.

[31] *Das sogenannte Böse*, 413.

[32] Ibid., 129.

[33] Ibid., 413.

[34] Ernst Bloch: "In the world, one must look after justice oneself, as

that God has entrusted the world to the decisions of men: *tradidit mundum disputationi eorum* (Qo 3:11). But that such a fantastic and, at bottom, despairing idea could be conceived at all and promulgated under the banner of hope, and that it should be seriously discussed—that fact alone indicates our abysmal degree of helplessness regarding our own historical future.

$$\sim$$

Even if claims like this cannot be taken at all seriously enough as symptoms, they nevertheless do not, by virtue of their explicit content, make us any wiser. And so it is with an enlivened sense of curiosity that one turns to *Teilhard de Chardin*, who, in his *opus magnum* on the phenomenon of man, comments specifically not only on the future of man but also on his end as well as the earth's, *la Terre Finale*.[35] Although his aim is to speak about this "without any element of apocalypse", that cannot mean that he is indifferent to the message of the Apocalypse. The special character of Teilhard's thought seems to me to lie precisely in the fact that for him—as opposed to what otherwise by no means seldom occurs in the case of scholar-priests —scholarship and spirituality do not remain two separate areas. His religious meditations are thoroughly in-

something to be expected and pursuable." *Zur Ontologie des Noch-Nicht-Seins*. Philosophische Grundfragen I (Frankfurt am Mainz, 1961), 40.

[35] *Phénomène*, 304ff.

terfused with scientific knowledge; when speaking at a religious wedding ceremony, he refers to the "God of evolution", or when a friend's son comes to him with personal religious problems, he responds to him —from nine in the evening till midnight while wandering the streets of Paris in drenching rain—by talking "of Christ's active role in the development of the cosmos".[36] Of course, we are expressly focusing our attention here on just one question among many in his total worldview. Condensed into summary—indeed, almost inadmissibly summary—form, that worldview is something like this: the material of the universe, in its ever-increasing complexity and consciousness, is becoming more and more intensely concentrated into itself, with man being the extreme forefront of this process, including man as a social entity, which seems to be finally growing capable of a collective thinking whose essential goal, the Omega Point of reason, is to become identical with the universal Cosmic Christ, in whom ultimately the whole of evolution will show itself to be a process of becoming one with God:[37] cosmogenesis ultimately tends, via biogenesis and noogenesis, toward Christogenesis,[38] toward becoming Christ

[36] Ladislaus Boros, "Evolutionismus und Anthropologie", *Wort und Wahrheit* 13 (1958): 16.

[37] As he himself represents his views; cf. "La pensée de Teilhard de Chardin".

[38] Cf. his last diary entry, written three days before his death (April 7, 1955); it appears in P. Teilhard de Chardin, *L'avenir de l'homme* (Paris, 1959), 404f.

under the effective presupposition that "the mystical Christ has not yet attained his full growth".[39] Now, we are focusing, as I said, on only a tiny segment of this total conception that spans millions of years and asking just what form, in the opinion of Teilhard de Chardin, we ought to imagine the *final phase* of the history of humanity on this earth as taking. The answer that we receive to this is in some degree surprising.[40] It suggests, namely, that *two* kinds of hypothetical model are equally possible, although each is almost opposed to the other.

The *first* model looks, in the words of Teilhard de Chardin, like this. In the earth's final stage, evil, *le Mal*, will be reduced to a minimum; hunger and sickness, in their worst forms, will no longer need to be feared, for science will have overcome them; subdued by feeling for the earth and for humanity, *par le sens de la Terre et le sens humain*, hatred and internal conflict will also have vanished, under the ever-warmer rays of Omega. A certain unanimity will obtain in the whole intellectual-spiritual sphere. The ultimate process of convergence, while taking place under extreme tension, will nevertheless occur peacefully. That, then, is the first possible hypothesis—formulated, incidentally, in terms that strike me as almost alarmingly vague. However, Teilhard not only says of this model that it gives expression to hopes whose realization would justify every kind of effort; he also says that it "would" undoubtedly accord

[39] *L'avenir de l'homme*, 397.
[40] *Phénomène*, 320ff.

67

with "theory" in the best way conceivable. The hypothetical mode of expression here is rather strange, for by "theory" nothing seems likely to be meant but his own evolutionary conception!

The *second* model would thus apparently conform less well to theory, although it, too, is not just conceptually but actually possible. According to it, the final stage of history would look like this. Along with the good, evil increases as well, ultimately attaining, in a specifically new form, the utmost power. Humanity's energy becomes divided; acceptance of Omega and rejection of it stand opposed; an inner schism continues to widen within consciousness. An irreconcilable conflict splits the intellectual-spiritual sphere into two zones, each centering around its "contraposed pole of worship". Regarding this second hypothesis—for which, astonishingly, Teilhard himself goes on to cite further arguments—he says that it is more in agreement "with traditional apocalypses". Here, albeit in rather suspect (weakening and relativizing) plural form, he has thus himself used the disclaimed term "apocalypse"! This gloomy conception of the final stage of history, however, accords so little with his own evolutionary "theory" that one cannot but ask whether the two are not mutually exclusive, whether that second model, if it actually implies something that is a real possibility, does not make the theory simply collapse.

In Teilhard's interpretation just of the *present* human epoch, whose nihilistic aspects could, of course, hardly have remained hidden from him (he remarks on this in a section headed "Demands of the Future")[41]—already in that context, an idea crops up that seems difficult to reconcile with his total evolutionary conception. He talks of a "strike" that threatens to occur, and already shows signs of beginning, in the "intellectual-spiritual sphere". By this, he means something with far more radical implications, and something much more fundamental, than the technical possibility of man's self-extermination through atomic weapons (a possibility that, by the way, is strangely never discussed, as far as I know, in Teilhard's work). No, the danger that is growing "behind the modern unrest" consists in the possibility that "the elements of the world, because they think, will refuse to serve the world; or more exactly, that the world itself, inasmuch as it knows itself reflectively, will deny itself".[42] Whatever one might think of this truly staggering prognosis, it must nonetheless be admitted that such a "strike" can no longer be readily explained as being an evolutionary phenomenon. Teilhard, however, actually considers this possible; he reduces that act of self-negation, performed in the full clarity of reflective thought, to the level of an ailment and almost of the biological; he speaks of an "organic crisis of evolution".[43]

But that position, it seems to me, is thoroughly implausible in relation to the "paroxysm" of evil[44] and

[41] Ibid., 254: "Exigences d'Avenir".
[42] Ibid., 255.
[43] Ibid.
[44] Ibid., 321.

69

"ecstasy of discord"[45] that he says are to be expected in the final period. Formulations of this sort of notion, by the way, occur throughout Teilhard's entire work —yet they receive little mention in public discussions, where the tendency is to identify this thinker (whose ideas cannot be reduced to some easy formula) solely with an image of unquestioned enthusiasm about the future. However, in a brief work written in Tientsin in 1924, he already mentions the profound schism, the *schisme profond*, by which man will be rent in the final days: one side devotes itself to aims that are beyond it in order to achieve final real mastery of the world, while the other waits fervently for the demise of the world so as to be taken up with Christ into God.[46] This extreme form of negation, this fundamental split in the intellectual-spiritual sphere, cannot possibly, in my opinion, be numbered among those mere "aberrations" that Teilhard says come about as "by-products" (*sous-produits*) in the course of noogenesis.[47] In short, the implication of all this is that the conceptual structure underpinning the evolutionary worldview simply and finally collapses.

Apart from all formal inconsistencies, what nevertheless remains admirable about Teilhard de Chardin seems to me to be this: despite his systematic approach, he does not hesitate to speak about, and direct attention to, the sort of future whose advent is foreshad-

[45] Ibid., 322.

[46] *L'avenir*, 402.

[47] *Phénomène*, 347.

owed by the reality of historical man himself. Without exception (as he literally says), it has been a valid law, at least in the past, that evil increases in matching proportion to increases in good.[48] He refuses to suppress this possibility or to dress it up ideologically simply for the sake of "theory"; rather, he expects both himself and his reader to confront it without dissemblance, even if reason, with its need to make sense of everything, becomes helpless and falls silent.

~

However, when Teilhard says that the first-mentioned eschatological hypothesis (the one more readily conformable with "theory"), and it alone, is the expression of human hope, then the question arises of whether the alternative, less optimistic model of the end of history might nonetheless be equally capable of arousing hope.

Earlier on, we asked the question: Is the hope of man of such nature such as to be satisfiable at all within the realm of history? We therefore now need to ask: Is the history of man perhaps of such nature as to offer no grounds for hope?

[48] Ibid., 321.

IV

In both scope and depth, the most penetrating statement on the topic of "hope" to be found in present-
day literature is undoubtedly the work of *Ernst Bloch*.
The subject that has motivated his activity as a writer,
for more than fifty years now, is expressed in the title
of an early book from 1918, *Geist der Utopie* (Spirit of
utopia). In a postscript added by the author to the new
edition of that work in 1963, he expressly confirms the
continuity of that leading theme throughout all the
works published in the meantime, up to his comprehensive concluding work, written in exile, *Das Prinzip
Hoffnung* (The principle of hope). The identity and
uniformity of the basic idea signify, however, anything
but monotony. One need only scan the table of con-
tents of the book on hope, and page through it a bit,
in order to appreciate the unexpected, almost unmas-
terable, kaleidoscopic profusion of the concrete things
discussed in it: from the daydreams of children playing
hide-and-seek; through the new dress in the brightly
lit shop window, the "happy ending" of the popular
movie, the Mozartian opera, social utopias from Plato
to Marx, the wish structure implicit in fairy tales, the

celestial rose of the Dantean *Commedia*, the aria on longing from *Mignon*, Don Quixote, the fugue in Bach; Lao Tzu, Confucius, Buddha, and Mohammed; and up to the Marxian atheism of the kingdom of freedom. The whole thing is written, moreover, in a thoroughly nontechnical, directly human language, fueled by the author's passionate devotion to his subject matter, and with a sonority and polyphony of diction that both fascinate from the first moment on (especially for the first moment!) and are not usually to be encountered elsewhere in philosophical writings. The "other side of the coin", of course, is also implicit in these observations. It is by no means easy to ascertain, both on the whole and in particular, just what, "specifically and exactly", is actually being maintained; this difficulty extends even to the most centrally relevant concepts, including that of "hope" itself. "Music resounding in the shaft of the soul"—this phrase from Hegel, which Bloch retrospectively applies to his own early work,[1] is also quite apposite to his later, major work on hope, in which, for example, the following terms, used almost synonymously and strung together in a few lines, are invoked to characterize the object of hope: "happiness; freedom; nonalienation; golden age; land of milk and honey; the eternal feminine; the trumpet signal in *Fidelio*; the conformity with Christ on the day of Resurrection".[2] As we can see, references

[1] *Geist der Utopie* (Frankfurt am Mainz, 1964), 347.
[2] *Prinzip Hoffnung*, 1627.

to Bloch's "dream-hued" language are not unjustified. But precisely the quality thus extolled makes it nearly impossible to present his basic ideas in what must be, at best, a highly condensed summary and to discuss them critically. Nevertheless, that has to be attempted here.

Bloch likes to describe his *opus* as an "encyclopedia", i.e., as a comprehensive survey of human images of hope. This aspect of his undertaking is, in fact, both the most convincing and the least problematic one. It should also be discussed first here, which implies, then, discussing an attempt to elucidate what is actually being hoped for in the hopes of men. Bloch himself says that he is concerned with interpreting "dreams of a better life".[3] What, then, do people mean by a "better life", or, as Bloch modulates that term, by a "perfect"[4] or a "full"[5] life, and by a "full existence"?[6] They mean "a world without disappointment";[7] "coming home";[8] "bliss of a kind never known before";[9] "absolute satisfaction of needs";[10] "peace, freedom, and bread";[11] "heaven on

---

[3] Ibid., 9.
[4] Ibid., 1616.
[5] Ibid., 15.
[6] Ibid., 1194.
[7] Ibid., 1162.
[8] Ibid., 6.
[9] Ibid., 122.
[10] Ibid., 1565f.
[11] Ibid., 680.

earth";[12] "the world a homeland for man";[13] "the world to become like a house";[14] "restoration of humanity";[15] a world in which "men" are "men to each other"[16] and not wolves; "*regnum humanum*",[17] and "identity between man become one with himself and his world become a success for him".[18]

I said that this encyclopedically intended "inventory" was the least problematic aspect of Bloch's work; still, even it is already questionable; one need only consider what has obviously been left out or what has been accented. Take, for example, the last-cited item: "identity between man become one with himself and his world become a success for him"—this, Bloch says, is the "most hoped for object of hope, called the highest good";[19] it is the "all" that was formerly "conceived of", "mythologically", as "heaven".[20] Man's having become one with himself and with a world that has turned out well can, of course, mean many things. I would not even find it hard to construe this formulation—and equally well the other, albeit rather unusual, one about "absolute satisfaction of needs"—in a way consistent with reference to eternal beatitude.

---

[12] *Erbschaft dieser Zeit* (Frankfurt am Mainz, 1962), 157.

[13] *Prinzip Hoffnung*, 390.

[14] *Ontologie des Noch-Nicht-Seins*, 39.

[15] *Prinzip Hoffnung*, 679 (quoted from Marx).

[16] Ibid., 390.

[17] Ibid., 1618.

[18] Ibid., 364, 368.

[19] Ibid., 368.

[20] Ibid., 364.

Why not? But Bloch presumes to know that precisely this sort of interpretation must be excluded; his very inventory is restricted, as he himself puts it, to what is "nonillusionary"[21] in images of hope. To be sure, it makes little difference whether he also speaks of the "kingdom of heaven" and "attaining heavenly bliss";[22] what he means by this is nothing more than "heaven *on earth*".[23] He even speaks—no differently from Kant —of the "kingdom of God", but that is the "kingdom of God—without God".[24] Again, the biblical notion of the "Kingdom" is one of his fundamental, constantly recurring concepts; but "the utopia of the kingdom" "presupposes precisely that no God remains on high, given that none is, or ever was, there anyway".[25] "The world has no 'great beyond' ",[26] and "what is fixed high above [is] precisely untruth".[27] Although the latter comment is quite correct if directed against the deist-progressivist notion of an "extramundane God" (which, however, is rejected as much by the great tradition of Western theology[28] as by Ernst Bloch), this fundamentally proclaimed atheism nevertheless natu-

[21] Ibid., 16.

[22] *Geist der Utopie*, 343.

[23] *Erbschaft dieser Zeit*, 157.

[24] *Prinzip Hoffnung*, 1413.

[25] Ibid., 1524.

[26] Ibid., 1303.

[27] *Tübinger Einleitung in die Philosophie II* (Frankfurt am Mainz, 1964), 176.

[28] For example, "It must be the case that God is present in all things, and indeed, in the innermost way" (Thomas Aquinas, *Summa theo-*

rally extends, by implication, to every conceivable understanding of God.

What, then, is the situation here? The very first step, namely, the attempt to identify, in a comprehensive inventory, all the kinds of hope that are actually held by men, is made questionable from the start because the range of what can be hoped for is restricted to things realizable within this world; everything else is excluded from consideration on the grounds of being "illusory". In one respect, by the way, Bloch is quite right here: while we can wish for the most impossible things, we can hope only for what is possible. But who is authorized to pronounce on what is "possible" and what is not? In any case, Christianity —which, after all, empirically exists—maintains (and substantially defines itself in so doing) that it is no illusion to hope for "eternal life",[29] for the "resurrection of the dead", and also, put quite plainly and without qualification, for "heaven". Yet Bloch's encyclopedia, despite its otherwise "polyphonic" aspect, says nothing about these images of hope—a point that could not be argued with him apart from mutual clarification, several levels deeper, of certain prior, more fundamental questions.

---

logica I, 8, i). Cf. also Josef Pieper, *Wahrheit der Dinge*, 4th ed. (Munich, 1966), 54f.

[29] "Eternal life", by the way, is by no means an exclusively Christian object of hope; Plato, too, undoubtedly recognized it. Cf. Friedrich von Hügel, *Eternal Life. A Study of Its Implications and Applications* (Edinburgh, 1912).

But Ernst Bloch does not let things rest with assuming that human hope, insofar as it really deserves that name, is in fact directed exclusively toward what can be realized in this world. Beyond this, he is also convinced that what is hoped for can be realized only through "socialist transformation of the world".[30] "In dreams of a better life", a kind of "becoming happy" has "always" been "implicitly sought" that "cannot be ushered in except by Marxism";[31] "everything nonillusory in these images of hope tends toward Marx";[32] Marxism is "the reclamation of the good core of utopia";[33] it is "the human vision in realized form".[34]

It seems to me that one would, indeed, be quite right to listen to what Bloch has to say about the future dimension of the world, about the impossibility of a purely "static concept of being",[35] and about the "ontology of what is not yet in being"—so as perhaps to attain, in this way, a new understanding of that archetypically possessed, but long-forgotten, wisdom about our "existence as wayfarers".[36] But one

---

[30] *Prinzip Hoffnung*, 16.

[31] Ibid.

[32] Ibid.

[33] *Erbschaft dieser Zeit*, 151.

[34] *Prinzip Hoffnung*, 1608.

[35] Ibid., 17.

[36] In this connection, the orthodox party critics are right when they call Bloch's attention to the "concurrences and common elements" (naturally regarded as definitively compromising) that link him to certain streams of "present-day bourgeois philosophy in France and West Germany". It was not without a smile that I read the following words

should have no illusions about the fact that such things are only preliminaries for Bloch. Equally, it is not sufficient to see him as a mere representative of Marxism as an "idea" or socialism as a kind of "worldview", which questions could then undoubtedly be debated at length. (Who, incidentally, would not be a "socialist" if socialism really amounted to nothing but the ideal objective that men should be men, rather than wolves, to each other?) What concerns Bloch, however, is Marxism as a political reality. It is not as if that might not also be the subject of "debates" but just that one must be clear about exactly what is under discussion.

---

by Manfred Buhr ("Der religiöse Ursprung und Charakter der Hoffnungsphilosophie Ernst Blochs", *Deutsche Zeitschrift für Philosophie* 6 [1958]: 595ff.): "As early as 1935, a book appeared by the Catholic philosopher Josef Pieper . . . that attempts to demonstrate, through reversion to Thomas Aquinas and critical analysis of Heidegger's *Sein und Zeit*, that hope is a central motif in philosophy (*Über die Hoffnung* [Leipzig, 1935]). There we read: 'The sole response that corresponds to the actual existential situation of man is hope.' Hope, in the formulation that follows a bit later, 'is the sole virtue of the not yet in being'. Here, it is at least . . . noticeable that Pieper, just like Bloch, views hope as a distinct basic attitude . . . and relates it to the not yet in being. Something similar can be observed in the leader of Catholic existentialism in France, Gabriel Marcel." The "tragic" thing, this passage by Manfred Buhr concludes, is that Bloch "does not seem at all aware of" the relationship between these ways of thinking. Now, I do not regard it as "tragic" that Bloch is unaware of certain publications; but I do find it disturbing that whole areas of the great Western ontological and anthropological tradition, in which a "closed and static concept of being" never enjoyed any validity, have remained unknown to him.

Bloch thus speaks expressly of "those countries where Marxism has come to power"; in them alone, "the daydream of the *regnum humanum*" is "no longer up in the air or in heaven".[37] The Soviet Union—we are told in unmistakable terms—is the place where that which Joachim of Fiore meant by the Third Age has begun to be realized, a fact that is, however, "not understood by the forces of darkness".[38] And nowhere other than in the "construction of communism" does "the content of the kingdom of freedom" find its initial realization;[39] prior to that, it was "still not present anywhere".[40] The most extreme formulation of this idea occurs, remarkably enough, in the section of the book on hope that deals with the political role of Judaism in the world. Bloch understands that role in a

[37] *Prinzip Hoffnung*, 1618f.

[38] Ibid., 596.

[39] Ernst Bloch knows as well as everyone else, of course, that precisely in "those countries where Marxism has come to power" (*Prinzip Hoffnung*, 1618f.) freedom is an extremely problematic matter; in the end, it was not wholly by coincidence that he preferred Tübingen University to the one in Leipzig. That lends all the more weight to what he has to say about this problem area; hence, I cite an extract from the chapter on "Freedom and Order": "Not without reason is Marxism also animated, along with what one might call the element of tolerance that is expressed in the kingdom of *freedom*, by what one might call the element of the cathedralistic that is expressed precisely in the *kingdom* of freedom, in freedom as a *kingdom*. The paths to this are . . . not liberal; they are seizure of power in the state, they are discipline, authority, central planning, the party line, orthodoxy. . . . It is precisely total freedom . . . that wins through in the will to orthodoxy" (*Prinzip Hoffnung*, 618).

[40] Ibid., 241.

strongly ethical, if not even religious, sense. Judaism signifies "not only a more or less anthropological quality" "but [also] a certain Messianic passion, one for the authentic Canaan";[41] "the only question is this: do the Jews . . . , as such, still have a consciousness of what the God of Exodus said to his servant Israel, not as a promise but as a task: 'I have imparted my spirit to him; he will bring justice to the heathens' ".[42] In view of this interpretation, and only in view of it, one understands how Bloch can say,[43] of all things, that precisely what is realistic in hope, what is "fully and utterly nonfanciful", is expressed in this passage from the Psalms: "If I forget you, O Jerusalem, let my right hand wither!" (Ps 137:5). Where—so one thinks—is to be found here even a trace of possible atheism or confinement to the empirical here-and-now? Nonetheless, it is precisely this great mystical name "Jerusalem" that Bloch unreservedly invokes—in a moving and absolutely committed polemic against Zionism (and, incidentally, also the state of Israel)—as providing the political foundations of Marxism: "As much of Judaism's prophetic heritage as exerts a continuing influence and makes it uniquely important . . . has been given contemporary form . . . by Marx."[44] And then comes that extreme formulation that I am concerned with here; in it, in the most outrageous way, Jerusalem and

41 Ibid., 709.
42 Ibid., 712.
43 *Ontologie des Noch-Nicht-Seins*, 38.
44 *Prinzip Hoffnung*, 705.

Lenin are posited as identical: it reads: "*Ubi Lenin, ibi Jerusalem!*"[45]

His position could not, it seems to me, be expressed more avowedly, more aggressively, more plainly, and also, in a certain sense, more shockingly: what is connoted by everything that man, informed by inner experience as well as tradition, could at all sensibly hope for, and thus by the comprehensive totality of what is both able to be hoped for and worth hoping for, is, logically and actually, not just what can be realized purely in this world; rather, such realization is also ultimately achievable only through political and social activity, and indeed, more precisely, through "socialist transformation of the world" such as has already begun with the Marxist revolution.

Naturally, the questions that arise here are legion. Is it really true, for example, viewed in terms of the factually historical, that "everything nonillusory in these images of hope" has been taken up into Marxism? I regard that as demonstrably false and also, incidentally, as a clear instance of the "wishful thinking" that Bloch otherwise so passionately opposes. Further, it must be asked whether this turn toward the purely political, and thus toward what can be planned and produced, does not covertly distort the original sense of the concept of "hope". Is not the aim of describing and elucidating what is to be hoped for supplanted by a program of practical action, of changing and producing things?

[45] Ibid., 711.

Not the least objection can be made, of course, to such a program "in itself", which can be something entirely sensible and necessary. And yet it is possible that, through it, precisely that which is intimated to us by the indwelling wisdom of language itself becomes drowned out: namely, that it is obviously characteristic of men by nature, as those who truly hope, to be directed toward fulfillment of just the kind that they cannot bring about themselves.

～

A far weightier sort of misgiving is that, in all these expectations about the future, regardless of whether they have arisen on the basis of an idealist philosophy of progress, of evolutionism, or of social religions, mention is hardly even once made of *death*. I am referring here not so much to the philosophical interpretation of this major theme, i.e., not to a "metaphysics of death" or anything of that sort. In that vein, death is certainly spoken about in the work of Ernst Bloch; at bottom, however, his remarks on this "mightiest non-utopia"[46] amount to nothing more than the deceptive notion of an "extra-territoriality toward death", to the old and familiar sophism (grown no more convincing in the meanwhile) about "non-encounterability"—since, after all, "when the person exists, death does not; and when death exists, the person does not".[47] Teilhard

[46] Ibid., 1297.
[47] Ibid., 1391.

84

de Chardin, too, speaks of death, even if in a fairly incidental way: it is "a necessary functional element in the mechanism and upward movement of life".[48] But this is not the kind of thing that my misgiving pertains to; nor does it have anything to do, I believe, with what Karl Rahner has criticized as "Western humanism's extreme sensitivity about death".[49] Rather, I am talking about the simple fact that we, those who hope, will die before the golden age will have dawned—the golden age, the ascent of life, the eternal peace, the kingdom of freedom, the "heaven on earth".

At the earlier-mentioned symposium on the future of man,[50] a physician from the University of Pennsylvania (who, upon closer inspection, proves to be an emigrant Pole, and thus carries the burden of old Europe on his shoulders)—this professor of medical research, Hilarius Koprowski, ironically called into question, with one drastic admonition, all the planning for the future that blossomed so excessively in the evolutionary climate of that convention: "*It is funny, you will be dead someday.*"[51] And he calls to mind the ancient gravestone inscription *Et in Arcadia Ego*, which means not at all "I, too, was born in

[48] *Phénomène*, 346.
[49] "Christlicher Humanismus. Vortrag auf der Tagung der Paulus-Gesellschaft (April 1966)", *Orientierung* 30 (1966): 119.
[50] *Man and His Future*, 214f.
[51] A quote from e. e. cummings, "Sonnets—Actualities", II in *Complete Poems* (New York: Harcourt Brace Jovanovich, 1972).

Arcadia",[52] but rather "even in Arcadia I (death) am present."

Thus the radically profound question is broached about just what significance can be attached to the golden age, to a "world without disappointment", to "man's having become one with himself" (and so on) as long as there is death. How do things stand regarding our hopes if we nevertheless must die? Hope is directed toward salvation, but "salvation is nothing if it does not deliver us from death".[53] This latter sentence from the writings of Gabriel Marcel is wholly and utterly clear to me, whereas I cannot understand a single word of what Ernst Bloch says on this subject, namely, that the "certainty of class consciousness [is] . . . a *novum* against death",[54] an "herb against death".[55] It is correct enough that "the class" does not die, no more than does society, the cosmos, or even "evolution"; it is solely the personal individual whose fate is to die. But this very fact also provides the basis for that totally unbreakable relationship that binds death and hope to one another: it is absurd to think that a collective entity (the human species, the universe, nature) might be capable of hoping; that would be, at best, a merely figurative, inadequate use of words. Strictly considered, hope, no differently from death,

[52] So reads the opening line of Schiller's poem *Resignation* (1786).

[53] Gabriel Marcel, *The Mystery of Being*, Gifford Lectures 1949–1950, II. *Faith and Reality* (Chicago: Henry Regnery, 1951), p. 180.

[54] *Prinzip Hoffnung*, 1380.

[55] Ibid., 1383.

exists only as the act of a person. Naturally, it is not to be expected that death could ever be removed from the world. And the claim is obviously incorrect that it is senseless to hope as long as the one who hopes must physically die.

What I insist on, however, is this: no conception of a future state of affairs that just ignores the fact of death, that thus simply fails to take into consideration not only the man who lives toward death, who is destined for death, but also those who have already died, the dead—no such image of the future can seriously be put forward as being in any sense an object of human hope! How can one speak of hope when what is hoped for is conceived in such a way that it could not at all be granted to the very being that is solely capable of hoping, namely, the individual, the particular person?

This individual can, of course, entertain speculative ideas about the sorts of thing that men might, say, a few hundred years from now, be pursuing on this earth: interplanetary space flights, electronic information technology, prolongation of the average life span by a decade or perhaps more. And this individual might well become honestly enthusiastic about these conjectures, purely from a delight in technical perfection, in human boldness and inventiveness, or in successful experimentation. However, insofar as he is one who hopes, all this is, strictly considered, of no relevance to him. It bears on his curiosity and his interest in speculation, but in what sense is he supposed to be able to put his hope in such future achievements? One who hopes, after all, is not one who desires to know something but is rather one who anticipates some real thing; one who hopes is concerned about being granted something that he regards as good. And that good thing would thus have to be obtainable even on the other side of death.

Everyone is familiar with polemical talk of "consolation in the hereafter". This expression occurs frequently in the works of Ernst Bloch;[56] its use is related to that of "opium of the people" and signifies a "clerical construction"[57] that "[invokes] the just distribution of other-worldly goods in order to offset the unjust distribution of this-worldly goods";[58] what "consolation in the hereafter" means is that the exploited are diverted from active pursuit of their just demands by being referred to the joys of heaven.

Now, it is not my intention to claim that something like this has never occurred and might not possibly occur at any time. Nevertheless, one deprives himself of an indispensable insight if he insists on viewing the word "hereafter" as a purely deceptive term. "Hereafter", of course, is not primarily a noun but is rather an adverb (of time or place); what is involved here is not so much "the" hereafter, as if it resembled some region that could be surveyed or landscape that could be described; rather, it is something far less ambitious, namely, a term for the notion that there really is, re-

[56] Ibid., e.g., 592, 596, 1411, 1511.

[57] Ibid., 1411.

[58] Ibid., 1511.

gardless of what its precise nature might be, such a thing as a yonder shore. What is meant is the other side of death, and nothing else. The Greeks spoke quite unabashedly of what is "over there" (*ekeí*), by which they meant not only the "place" of the dead but also —as one can read in the dictionaries—their special mode of "enduring" and of "time". In short, what is meant by the term "hereafter" is precisely that concrete future that awaits us all. Whatever may be the case regarding the possibility of obtaining information about this (and of course everything depends on the legitimization and credibility of such information), the matter can nevertheless not fail to be of direct interest to me. In this respect, I am wholly on the side of simple, realist-oriented understanding, and not on that of abstract speculation and fantasy.

In any event, if there is no hope about the "hereafter" in the sense just described, i.e., hope that can be realized on the other side of death, then there is no hope at all. And as for the prospect that, after centuries have passed, there might possibly arise on earth a "classless" society or, in Kantian terms, "a civil society that universally effects justice",[59] or a new level of cosmogenesis and "universalization"[60]—such a prospect is really of concern to me, as one who hopes, only if I can think of it as being somehow linked to that hope in the "hereafter" that pertains to my very own

[59] Kant, *Gesammelte Schriften*, vol. 8, p. 22.

[60] Teilhard de Chardin, *L'Apparition de l'homme* (Paris, 1956), 367f.

destiny on the other side of death. Those decidedly "this-worldly" and purely intra-historical expectations about the future, by contrast, in which death and the future that awaits us all (and is "ours" in the strictest sense) have been simply left out of consideration—those visions of the future, and (in direct reversal of what is usually said) precisely those, are something like a "consolation in the hereafter": a completely abstract, deceptive consolation that refers men to something actually situated wholly and utterly "beyond" their concrete existences.

~

A final critical misgiving about all these idealistic, evolutionary, and Marxist visions of the future pertains to their *legitimization*. Only what is really possible, I said earlier, can be hoped for, whereas there are no limits to wishing. But what also distinguishes one who hopes is having to put up with being asked about the basis for his hope. In the case of wishing, it is sufficient to ask: *What* do you wish for? But in relation to hoping, the wording must be: What, and *on what grounds*? How does one know that humanity is actually advancing toward a state of intra-historical perfection—whether one happens to describe that state (with Giambattista Vico) as a rationally ordered universal republic or (with Kant) as a society regulated by civil law? On what basis can one be sure that "evolution" will triumphantly surmount the historical misery of man? By what cogent reasons can the expectation be supported that man's longing for a "full existence" will really be satisfied through intra-historical activity of this or that kind? How can one even claim to know that control over atomic energy, the very "grace of such immeasurable power", will "ultimately force" humanity "to order itself in accordance with law and justice"?[61]

What certainty is there, on the contrary, that the end of history will not come about—as Karl Jaspers[62] thinks "simple understanding" tells us—in the form of the self-annihilation, "in the approaching decades", of man? And Jaspers' voice is but one in an entire chorus that, as one can hardly dispute, at least gives expression to something of how this age of ours feels about the future. Reinhold Schneider's gloomy conviction of the "approaching end of history"[63] is well known: "Our age is the interlude between the end of the kingdom and the final tick of the clock."[64] Gabriel Marcel reports that Max Picard said (in conversation) almost the same thing: "Probably many of us will directly experi-

[61] Friedrich Dessauer, *Atomenergie und Atombombe* (Frankfurt am Mainz, [1948]), 294.

[62] "The situation is irrevocable: men can annihilate man and all life on earth by their own actions. Plain understanding tells them that it is likely that such an end will occur in the approaching decades." So says Karl Jaspers in the compilation *Wo stehen wir heute?* (Gütersloh, 1960), 41.

[63] *Winter in Wien* (Freiburg im Breisgau, 1958), 114.

[64] Ibid., 191.

ence the apocalyptic event."[65] Ernst Jünger writes, "In any case, things are now threatening that do not fit in with our view of history, and indeed, not even with the human epoch."[66] And in a letter written just after the horror of Hiroshima, Thomas Mann says, "The human situation is now more ominous than ever before. Yet nobody should presume to say how things could have been done better. . . . One begins to have doubts about the wisdom of creation. 'Thus it would have been better if nothing had been created.' "[67] Somewhat hesitantly, I add to this randomly chosen sequence an aphorism from the "unkempt thoughts" of the Pole Stanislaw Lec; but after all, this grim saying also reflects our epoch's sense of what is possibly to come: "I would have to laugh if they did not finish demolishing the world before the world ended."[68] (Admittedly, the following sentence occurs in the same work: "I cannot imagine the world's ending prior to the triumph of truth"[69]—regarding which I ask myself whether the notion of the "Last Judgment" might not imply exactly that: the simultaneity, indeed, the identity, of the "end of the world" and the "triumph of truth".)

Naturally, those making such negative speculations must also face up to the same question: How do you

[65] "Pessimismus und eschatologisches Bewußtsein", *Dokumente* 6 (1950): 54.

[66] *Der Weltstaat. Organismus und Organisation* (Stuttgart, 1960), 22f.

[67] *Briefe 1937–1947*, 438.

[68] *Neue Unfrisierte Gedanken* (Munich, 1964), 27.

[69] Ibid., 43.

know that? And the point also applies to them that no one can know anything at all about the historical future—unless one might be able to do so on the basis of intelligence that is prophetic in the strict sense.

The brighter expectations, on the one hand, and the darker ones, on the other, are, by the way, not so unambiguously classifiable as they might initially appear. For example, it might very well be the case that precisely the success of those big plans to create a universal *fulfillment society*[70] would be something to fear, or its success at least far more than its failure.[71]

Furthermore, reference has been made, with good reason, to the "inner dialectical relationship"[72] that links optimism about progress, and precisely it, to a philosophy of despair.

But that would also imply that people might possibly prepare themselves for catastrophe without this having to affect their hope in any way.

[70] Julian Huxley, in *Man and His Future*, 21.

[71] Ernst Jünger, *Weltstaat*, 57.

[72] Gabriel Marcel, *Ontologisches Geheimnis*, 38; similarly in *Philosophie der Hoffnung*, 64.

V

The question is: Can there be legitimate prophecy about history? Christianity answers this with a clear yes. For example, among its sacred texts is the prophetic book of Revelation (the Apocalypse), and in it (although not in it alone) there are assertions about the ultimate future of historical man—not so much, then, about how history will continue but rather about how it will end.

In this acceptance of a revealed prophecy about history, certain fundamental presuppositions are also taken for granted, the most important of which must be expressly stated if discussion of the topic "hope and history" is not to be an unpromising business from the very start. Above all, it is presupposed that human existence takes place wholly and utterly within the force field of an infinite, trans-historical, and "creative" reality; that what can be experienced of the here-and-now could never be identical with the totality of existence; and that rather (quite expectably and for that reason) the end, and also even the beginning, of human history as a whole and of individual biography, must necessarily remain beyond our empirical grasp. Another presupposition is that there is not only truth as known but also truth as believed; and thus information about reality that has its origin not in human thinking but in that trans-human sphere, to which, accordingly, one gains access (if at all) not through the use of one's own eyes and thought alone but rather—as not only Paul[1] but also Plato[2] says—*ex akoés*, by hearsay. It has recently been suggested[3] that a distinction should be made between "scientific" and "speculative" kinds of prognostication, the latter being defined by their "unalterable relationship to some central idea". Under this highly questionable category (which in any case is already established in the area of human speculation about history), prophecy is then subsumed. In reality, however, it has not the least in common with that. Prophecy either is divinely certified information or does not exist at all. On what other basis, incidentally, would it be likely to be supposed credible?

And yet theology, which could be defined as the attempt to interpret the documents of revelation and the sacred tradition based on them—Christian theology has, strangely enough, always maintained that religious truths, for all their communication through revelation, "nevertheless remain concealed"[4] to us; we

[1] Rom 10:17.

[2] *Phaedo*, 61 d 9.

[3] Wolfgang Wieser, "Der Mensch und seine Zukunft. Grenzen und Möglichkeiten wissenschaftlicher Prognosen", *Merkur* 20 (1966): 317.

[4] Matthias Joseph Scheeben, *Die Mysterien des Christentums*, ed. by Josef Höfer (Freiburg im Breisgau, 1941), 8f.

96

cannot translate divine discourse without remainder into the flat comprehensibility of human language; its fullness of meaning cannot be exhausted by any interpretation. But all this applies particularly markedly to prophecy, to *still not fulfilled* prophecy about history —which, by nature, is probably the most challenging form in which revelation can present itself to the human mind. To be sure, prophecy certainly speaks about coming events, about a future that cannot be calculated in advance by any speculative technique, but it does not straightforwardly describe what is to happen. One cannot read prophecy like a "wanted person" notice in which something previously unknown is made recognizable and identified by name, so that one could keep it in mind like a detailed image of a sought object and use it to make the future "present". On the contrary, the key that would render the encoded message readable is by no means plainly evident. John Henry Newman has even said that "the event is the true key to prophecy".[5] One is tempted to ask just what, then, prophecy is supposed to be good for. Here, Karl Rahner suggests that while prophecy does not, admittedly, turn the future into a "fixed quantity" that could be reckoned with as such, what is stated in prophecy nevertheless does cease to be one of those things "that don't hurt you because you don't know about them".[6]

[5] *Grammar of Assent* (London, 1892), 446. Cf. here Karl Rahner, *Schriften zur Theologie*, vol. 4, pp. 407, 410.

[6] *Schriften zur Theologie*, vol. 4, p. 409.

The impatience of wanting to know leads to that familiar kind of spurious apocalyptics in which there is, above all, an attempt to establish, or even a claim to know, the concrete "omens" and the precise where and when—in the process of which, however, the very thing that the prophecy was truly meant to teach us gets overlooked. The non-datability of the events is, in the view of the great theological tradition, itself a part of the prophetic message of the Apocalypse. When we hear talk today of the "approaching end of history", or when an otherwise quite cautious analyst like Alexander Rüstow[7] describes the present-day situation as "eschatological" "in the full apocalyptic sense of the word", then we can only repeat the dictum that Thomas Aquinas used against the apocalyptists of the thirteenth century; it runs as follows: "No period of time can be specified at all, neither a short one nor a long one, after which the end of the world could be expected."[8]

It is therefore a by no means insignificant demand that one makes on himself if he acknowledges as true a revealed prophecy about the ultimate future of historical man. One finds himself challenged to conceive as concordant what initially seemed contradictory: one is supposed to regard the ultimately indecipherable, namely, history, as nevertheless not inherently unintelligible or even confused; one is supposed to refrain

[7] *Ortsbestimmung der Gegenwart. Eine universalgeschichtliche Kulturkritik*, 3 vols. (Erlenbach, Zurich, Stuttgart, 1950–57), vol. 3, p. 524.

[8] *Contra impugnantes Dei cultum et religionem*, 3, 2, 5, no. 531.

not only from easily managed explanatory formulas but also from agnostic resignation; one is supposed, regarding the end of history, to respect, in faith, certain trans-empirical reports that claim to reveal the future while nevertheless not actually showing it and that, while not depriving what is to come of its futurity (indeed, while even reinforcing that), nevertheless lay claim to illumining the darkness of what lies ahead.

~

But just what is it that one gets to know, however en-cryptedly, by acknowledging the validity of apocalyp-tic prophecy? If a philosopher attempts to answer this, then he clearly no longer speaks in his "own proper capacity"—as little as does the Socrates of the Platonic *Symposium*, who retells what he had been told by Dio-tima, the prophetess from Mantinea. Yet the philo-sopher, even then, still speaks as himself, and what he expresses is his own conviction. And if he happens to believe these kinds of trans-empirical reports to be true, he would simply cease to philosophize with any existential earnestness at all from the moment that he excluded them from consideration. But regarding just the question of where the historical process in general is heading, it is clear that no one can even meaningfully pose and discuss that question—which is absolutely fundamental to all philosophy of history—without be-ing able to have recourse to trans-empirical prophetic intelligence. For this reason, we can expect nothing other than that precisely in philosophizing about history (and there more than anywhere else in the field of philosophy), everything must necessarily become false from the bottom up if the believed total conception is wrong—regardless of whether it is a matter of the dogmas of evolutionism or those of dialectical materialism.

Now, the first thing that apocalyptic prophecy gives us to understand is its confirmation of an insight that we could also have reached through our own independent thinking: human history will not arrive at its fulfillment by way of an unbroken, continuously progressing developmental process—regardless of how strongly "dialectical" that development is otherwise viewed as being (even revolutions would still occur within the continuity referred to here). Moreover, there is nothing to indicate, in as much of history as has become capable of being experienced by us, that human society would be able in this way (for example, through a radical redistribution of property) to attain a state of fulfillment. As already noted, however, the chasm that one would have to leap over here is of a completely different kind: it is the boundary line of death that separates historical humanity from its own fulfillment, and this boundary line sunders the continuity of that "development".

It remains true, of course, strictly considered, that it is not humanity but the personal individual who—and who alone—dies. Since, however, the being that exists for the sake of its own perfection is not the species but solely the person, and since human history as a whole can never be conceived as separate from the fates of particular individuals (if, on the other hand, it is not simply identical with that),[9] universal human history also contains, at its very core, death.[10] Even Teilhard de Chardin, who simply cannot succeed in being a completely "pure" evolutionist because he is so much influenced by the realism of traditional historical thought—even Teilhard speaks of a *point de dissociation*,[11] i.e., a kind of dissolution, which evolution on earth would have to go through in order to arrive at fulfillment.

This same topic is addressed much more clearly and cogently, it seems to me, by the late Kant, thirteen years after his *Kritik der reinen Vernunft* (Critique of pure reason), in the meditative and intricate essay (not easily reducible to a few central theses) on "Das Ende aller Dinge" (The end of all things)—by which he definitely means the end of human history.

Obviously—so the essay begins—this end would have to be conceived as analogous to the death of the human individual, which is customarily described,

[9] Cf. here Hans Urs von Balthasar, "Vom Sinn der Geschichte in der Bibel", in *Der Sinn der Geschichte*, ed. L. Reinach (Munich, 1961), 117.

[10] "For Christianity, this secular task is one always uncompleted, one that again and again ultimately fails. Because it always has, for each individual person, an absolute limit: death. And so Christianity asserts of universal history, too, that it, at its very core, also contains death." Karl Rahner, *Schriften zur Theologie*, vol. 5, p. 131.

[11] *Phénomène*, 304.

in "pious language", as a "passing from time into eternity". Implicit in this notion is something both "horrifying" and "attractive", for which reason one cannot refrain from "repeatedly turning one's fear-averted gaze back upon it".[12] Above all, however, this idea must probably be "interwoven in some wonderful way with universal human reason". Naturally, the process of transition from the temporal being of the historical world to direct participation—whatever its particular form—in God's "eternity" lies wholly and utterly beyond our power of imagination; that goes almost without saying. Reason, if left to its own devices here, is completely at the end of its competence when the very conceptual approach itself is not the competence of someone else. It is at least evident, however, that such a passage out of the temporal could in no case be conceived on the model of a continuous development; rather, it could sooner be conceived as a kind of dissolution—and so, once again, as analogous to human dying, which also seems more like destruction than like progress and fulfillment. And if fulfillment is really to come about through disintegration, then it will occur not only in a concealed way but also contrary to all appearances—as we in fact believe, after all, both of a "good" human death in general and particularly of that paradigmatic dying in the fullness of time, in which it was in no way to be seen what had nevertheless taken place in truth.

[12] *Gesammelte Schriften*, vol. 8, p. 327.

For anyone who reflects on this, a further, more important piece of information that apocalyptic prophecy has in store for us will perhaps lose a little, if not of its frightfulness, then at least of its seeming absurdity —the claim, namely, that, as seen from within time (this qualification is naturally decisive), human history will come to an end not simply with the triumph of the true and good, not with the "victory" of reason and justice, but with something that, once again, may be hardly distinguishable from catastrophe. And what is obviously being referred to here is not primarily a cosmic catastrophe or, as it were, a physical exhaustion of the forces of historical order but rather, on the contrary, a monstrous intensification of power—a pseudo-order to be sure—a universal tyranny of evil.

Strangely enough, this kind of gloomy expectation, which inclines one at first to rebellion, is by no means unfamiliar to modern historical consciousness. Friedrich Nietzsche, for example, who throughout his life was passionately interested in the subject of "the future" (his unfinished major work was originally to be titled *Das was kommt* [What is to come]) [13]—Nietzsche had noted, under the heading "Further Development of Man", a passage from Baudelaire that is found in the unpublished papers and refers to a menacing "phantom of order", supported by political power with the

[13] Cf. here Walter Bröcker, *Das was kommt, gesehen von Nietzsche und Hölderlin* (Pfüllingen, 1963), 5.

help of violent coercion, that "would make our contemporary humanity, insensitive though it has become,
shudder".[14] It is as in Franz Kafka's *Prozeß* (The trial):
"The lie is made into the world order." A modern
politician, Hermann Rauschning (relevantly qualified
through particularly intimate experience with the to-
talitarian regime), regards it as thoroughly possible[15]
that there could be a "world civilization of material
pleasure" "based on progressive dehumanization and
under a monopoly, preserved by a Universal Grand
Inquisitor, of . . . absolute power". The reference to a
Grand Inquisitor recalls the name of another European
who similarly presaged, with seismographic sensitivity,
what was obscurely announcing itself: Dostoyevsky. In
his tale of the Grand Inquisitor, in fact, the following
unsettling sentence can be found: "In the end they
will lay their freedom at our feet and say to us, 'Make
us your slaves, but feed us.' "[16]

[14] *Gesammelte Werke*, Musarion-Ausgabe (Munich, 1922ff.), vol. 16,
p. 401.

[15] *Die Zeit des Deliriums* (Zurich, 1948), 63.

[16] This sentence, by the way, is also quoted in a book by Aldous
Huxley that is well worth thinking about: *Brave New World Revisited*
(1958; rpt. London: TriadGrafton, 1983), p. 187. In 1931, under the
title *Brave New World* (which, incidentally, stems from Shakespeare's
The Tempest), Huxley had published a utopian novel (in the vein of
Orwell's *1984*) whose events are set in the sixth or seventh century
"A.F." (= after Ford). Thirty years later, the author looks back upon
that book: "In 1931 . . . I was convinced that there was still plenty of
time. The completely organized society, . . . the abolition of free will
by methodical conditioning, the servitude made acceptable . . . these
things were coming all right, but not in my time, not even in the time

But it is not modern visions of the future that should be discussed here now. Rather, the question still requiring discussion is what prophetic information might possibly be attainable about the end of history. Naturally, there would be little point in making inevitably dilettantish suggestions of one's own about how to interpret the Apocalypse. If, however, one questions modern scientific theology about, say, the topic of the "reign of the Antichrist", what one initially receives are quite sparsely worded answers. Not much evidence is available on that subject, says Karl Rahner.[17] Nonetheless, the little that is then said is clear enough. One speaks, for instance, of an antagonistic character of historical events that increasingly sharpens as the end approaches;[18] one expects that the final period will be marked by an extreme concentration of the energy of evil[19] and a previously unknown vehemence of the struggle against Christ and Christianity[20] (and "against everything good", as Thomas Aquinas had said);[21] or

of my grandchildren. . . . In this third quarter of the twentieth century A.D., . . . I feel a good deal less optimistic than I did [then]. . . . The prophecies made in 1931 are coming true much sooner than I thought they would", pp. 11–12.

[17] "Antichrist", in *Lexikon für Theologie und Kirche*, 2d ed. (1957ff.), vol. 1, col. 635f.

[18] Karl Rahner, *Schriften zur Theologie*, vol. 4, p. 425; vol. 5, p. 132.

[19] Paul Althaus, in *Religion in Geschichte und Gegenwart*, vol. 2, col. 688.

[20] *Handbuch theologischer Grundbegriffe*, ed. Heinrich Fries (Munich, 1963), vol. 1, p. 334.

[21] Commentary on the Second Letter to the Thessalonians, 2, 2.

one calls the *potentia saecularis*[22] of the Antichrist "the strongest world power in history".[23] All these formulations are almost literal quotations from present-day theology, both Protestant and Catholic. Their disturbing message is not easily ignored. It presents us, to be sure, with many other kinds of thing to consider; above all, however, it makes it impossible for us to conceive the end of earthly human history in such a way as to entail that a perhaps difficult and struggle-filled, but still constantly advancing, process of ascent will come to a harmonious and triumphant conclusion in it—even though this, according to the earlier-noted words of Teilhard de Chardin, would undoubtedly accord much better with "theory" and indeed equally well with idealist, Marxist, and evolutionist "theory".

In any case, the image of history conveyed by the Apocalypse—insofar as such can be spoken of at all—looks quite different, in every respect, from that. Since this conception takes account of human freedom to choose evil and also of "the" evil as a dark and demonic historical force—for that reason alone, dissension, breakdown, irreconcilable conflict, and even catastrophe cannot, in principle, be alien to the nature of human history, including its everyday course of events.

And yet this is not the last word of apocalyptic prophecy. Its last word, and its decisive report, all else

[22] Ibid.

[23] Ethelbert Stauffer, *Theologie des Neuen Testaments*, 3d ed. (Stuttgart, 1947), 192.

notwithstanding, is the following: a blessed end, infinitely surpassing all expectations; triumph over evil; the conquest of death; drinking from the fountain of life; resurrection; drying of all tears; the dwelling of God among men; a New Heaven and a New Earth. What all this would appear to imply about hope, however, is that it has an invulnerability sufficient to place it beyond any possibility of being affected, or even crippled, by preparedness for an intra-historically catastrophic end—whether that end be called dying, defeat of the good, martyrdom, or world domination by evil.

~

With that, all of our opening questions come thronging back; only now, in fact, do they present themselves in their full acuteness. Is human history, then, a "cause for despair" after all? Or what justification, and what sustenance, might it be able to provide for hope? Is it really part of the nature of human hope that it can never find satisfaction and fulfillment in the realm of history?

Basically, this last question has already been answered. If earthly existence itself is pervasively structured toward what is "not yet in being", and if a man, as a *viator*, is truly "on the way to" something right up to the moment of death, then this hope, which is identical with our very being itself, either is plainly absurd or finds its ultimate fulfillment on the other side of death, "after" the here-and-now. In a word, the object of existential hope bursts the bounds of "this" world.

Nevertheless, accusations of detached "other-worldliness" would miss the mark here, and for many reasons. The persuasiveness of those, however, is immediately evident only to someone who accepts Christian religious truth. This is not to imply that even Christians might not have false notions about hope and precisely about its other-worldliness; but then they would be misunderstanding themselves. Perhaps, however, even non-Christians can be reasonably asked, in this connection, to listen to, and reflect upon, arguments based on Christian self-understanding.

Hence: it is—point number one—precisely not, as Ernst Bloch says with Friedrich Engels,[24] a "distinctive 'history of the kingdom of God' " whose fulfillment Christians expect, i.e., one bypassing an "actual" history that has supposedly been declared inessential. Rather, vice versa, it is exactly this identical, created reality, here and now present before our eyes, whose fulfillment, in direct overcoming of death and catastrophe, we hope for as "salvation". The "kingdom of God" realizes itself nowhere other than in the very midst of this historical world. It is true, of course, that nobody can have an idea of what is concretely meant by "resurrection" and "a New Earth" as images of hope; but what else could those possibly imply if not this: that not one iota will ever be futile, or lost, of whatever is good in earthly history—good, just, true, beautiful, fine, and sound.

[24] *Prinzip Hoffnung*, 1411.

Above all, however—point number two—Christians are convinced that the boundary of death separating this world and the next has, in a certain sense, already been crossed from the farther side, namely, through the event that is covered by the technical theological term "Incarnation". One of the recurrent symbols through which men have, from time immemorial, attempted to make comprehensible the essential nature of what they hope for is the Great Banquet. Plato also refers to this, and that aspect of his thought should not, I believe, be forgotten. He speaks not only of a dwelling together, of a *synousia*,[25] of gods and men, but also expressly of a banquet in which the soul, outside of time and in a place beyond the heavens, takes part, as a tablemate of the gods, in satiating itself with contemplation of true being.[26] This could not be expressed much better even by Christians, and their expression of it is, after all, not essentially different. But Plato would never have been able to dream of *the* communal banquet in which Christianity recognizes and celebrates the real beginning and pledge of that blessed life at God's table. Since earliest times, it has been called *sýnaxis*, or *communio*.[27] This implies, however, that one fundamentally misunderstands and degrades this table community if it is not conceived and enacted as a community of persons with one another, and indeed, a community

[25] *Phaedo*, 111 b 7.

[26] *Phaedrus*, 247 a–e.

[27] Cf., for example, Thomas Aquinas, *Summa theologica* III, 73, 4, and *Scriptum in IV Libros Sententiarum*, 4 d 8 I i 3.

from which nobody can be excluded through arbitrarily drawn restrictions.

A more profound sort of grounding for human solidarity cannot, it seems to me, be conceived. But the reverse also holds true: wherever true human communion is realized, or even just longed for, this universal table community is, whether one knows and likes it or not, quietly being prepared—regardless of what, in any concrete case, the catchword might be: democracy, kingdom of freedom, classless society (with the sole proviso that dictatorship by oneself and discrimination against others is not also on the program, whereby everything would be spoiled from the start). The relationship to the topic of "hope" here is more direct than one might suppose. No matter where and by whom the realization of fraternity among men is understood and pursued as the thing that is truly to be hoped for, there exists, *eo ipso*, a subterranean link to the elementary hope of Christianity.

Christianity's major theological tradition has always maintained that any non-Christian who is filled with conviction that God—in some way deemed suitable by him—will set men free therefore also believes implicitly, *fide implicita*, in Christ;[28] such a person, even if without knowing it, is of the same mind as Christianity and belongs to its community. In precise correspondence to this, one should also, it seems to me,

---

[28] Thomas Aquinas, *Summa theologica* II, ii, 2, 7 ad 3; cf. also *Quaestiones Disp. de Veritate* 14, 11 ad 5.

speak of a *spes implicita*. Whoever, for instance, invests the power of his hope in the image of a perfect future human society, in which men are no longer wolves to each other and the good things of life are justly distributed—such a one participates, precisely thereby, in the hope of Christianity.

And just as *implicite* "believing" non-Christians often enough put professed Christians to shame by the vitality and seriousness of their faith, so they might possibly also surpass them in the passion of their hope, whose "religious" absoluteness ultimately just proves how much their expectations—perhaps contrary to their own proclaimed life agenda—are nevertheless basically directed toward something that cannot be brought about by any action "to change the world".

It is inherent in the nature of this situation itself that such common concerns are perceivable as such only from the standpoint of "explicit" hope. In other words, if Christianity does not see those common concerns and identify them by name, then no one will see them; above all, however, they will then remain mute and without historical force. How much there is to be done in this area hardly needs to be stated.

⁓

Still, commonness is not the same as identity, and the "distinctiveness of Christianity" also remains a perpetual task. In conclusion, something still needs to be said about one of these points of differentiation. It pertains to the non-specifiability of the object of hope.

Gabriel Marcel expressed the profound insight (referred to earlier here) that true hope pushes constantly beyond all the objects by which it is initially enkindled[29] and loses what is best in it as soon as one starts making "stipulations" or, indeed, even just tries to imagine its concrete object.[30] Not only are the date and the time of fulfillment unknown to us; we are likewise not given to know the form in which it will realize itself and be conferred upon us.[31] Thus it is characteristic of those who truly hope that they remain open to the possibility of a fulfillment that surpasses every preconceivable human notion.[32] And they will apply the energy of their hearts not so much to militant implementation of predefined plans and goals or eschatological images of order (through which human solidarity has already been often enough marched into the ground) as to the everyday accomplishment, in each given situation, of what is wise, good, and just. Precisely that is probably the true, and most human, form of historical activity. This supposition has noth-

[29] *Homo viator*, 43.

[30] Ibid., 60.

[31] Cf. Karl Rahner, *Schriften zur Theologie*, vol. 5, p. 173.

[32] Since prayer of supplication is nothing other than an expression of hope, and possibly the most adequate one of all ("*petitio est interpretativa spei*": Thomas Aquinas, *Summa theologica* II, ii, 17, 2, obj. 2), exactly the same thing holds true of those who pray in the right way. They, too, remain open to the possibility of a gift ultimately unknown to them; and if the concrete object of their supplication is not granted them, they nevertheless remain certain of the nonfutility of their prayer.

ing to do with timid, petit bourgeois aversion to the radical thrust of great political decisions, and certainly nothing to do with any kind of lack of trust in the historical future. It may well, however, have something to do with mistrust of any delimiting specification of the object of human hope.

The reason for that mistrust was expressed in very successful form, and also—precisely because of its avoidance of any all too clearly positive terminology —in a form especially adequate to its object, by Konrad Weiß. It comes to this: all attempts to construct a ready-made image of the future of historical man are burdened by the grave discrepancy that "it is not humanity that is the goal of the Incarnation".[33]

---

[33] The quote comes from an essay, so far unpublished, left by Konrad Weiß and entitled "Logos des Bildes" (Logos of the image).

INDEX

"aggressive drive", 63
Anders, Gunther, 16
Antichrist, 61, 105–106
anticipation, 31
apocalypse, 16, 53, 68,
    100; *see also* catastrophe
Apocalypse (Revelation),
    65, 95, 98, 105–7
atomic power, 48, 63

Balthasar, Hans Urs von,
    45, 101
Banquet, the Great, 109
Baudelaire, Charles-Pierre,
    103
belief, 96
Bloch, Ernst, 17–18, 53,
    64–65, 73–86, 88, 108
Brugger, Walter, 34
Buhr, Manfred, 18, 80

catastrophe, 61, 93, 103,
    106, 108
certitude, 21
changing world, 79, 111
Christ, 66–67, 70, 110
class consciousness, 86
classless society, 89, 110
communio, 109–110

communism, 81
confidence, 21
Congar, Yves, 45
"consolation in the
    hereafter", 88, 90
Conzelmann, Hans, 19
Cuénot, Claude, 37

death, 84–90, 100–102,
    108–9
deism, 77
despair, 25–26, 31, 107
Dessauer, Friedrich, 92
dialectical materialism, 53,
    100
disappointment, 25–26,
    28–30
distinctiveness of Chris-
    tianity, 111
Dostoyevsky, Fyodor
    Mikhaylovich, 104

Eichendorff, Joseph von,
    22
end of history, 59, 65–68,
    91–92, 95, 105–7
Engels, Friedrich, 108
"eternal content", 46
eternal life, 78

eternity, 46, 102
evil, 40–41, 67, 69–71,
  103–107
evolution:
  evolutionism, 64–66,
    100
  in science, 42, 62
  in Teilhard de Chardin,
    64–71
  of the cosmos, 42, 53–
    54
  vs. history, 35–40, 47–
    48
existentialism, 46, 80
expectation, 20–21
"extramundane God", 77

fide implicita, 110
forecasting, 48–51, 96; see
  also prophecy
freedom, 29–30, 34, 39–
  42, 48, 81
French revolution, 13, 55,
  57, 60
Fucks, Wilhelm, 48
future, 46–47, 51–53, 60–
  62, 65, 90, 98, 103,
  113

God, "being ashamed of",
  55
golden age, 85–86
good, 20
guilt, 34, 41

heaven, 78
"heaven on earth", 75–
  78, 85
Hegel, Georg Wilhelm
  Friedrich, 56, 74
Heidegger, Martin, 80
hereafter, 88–90
history:
  definition of, 33–34
  "human", 34
  vs. evolution, 35–40
Hoffmeister, Johannes, 21
hope:
  definition of, 19–28
  espérance, 26
  espoir, 26
  "fundamental", 27–28
Huxley, Aldous, 104–5
Huxley, Julian, 93

Incarnation, 109, 113

Jaspers, Karl, 91
Jerusalem, 81–83
Joachim of Fiore, 81
joy, 21–22
Judaism, 81–82
Judgment of the world, 46
Jünger, Ernst, 92
Jungle, 45–46

Kafka, Franz, 104
Kant, Immanuel, 13–15,
  41, 54–61, 90, 101
Kierkegaard, Søren, 14

kingdom of God, 46, 54–55, 108–110
"kingdom of man", 76, 81, 108
Koprowski, Hilarius, 85

Landsberg, Paul Ludwig, 26
Last Judgment, 92
Lec, Stanislaw, 92
linguistic usage, 19–20, 25–26
longing, 20
Lorenz, Konrad, 16, 40, 63–64

man as wayfarer: *see status viatoris*
Mann, Thomas, 55, 92
Marcel, Gabriel, 24, 28, 80, 86, 93, 112
martyrs, 35–36
Marxism, 18, 54, 64, 79–84
morality, 59–60
Muller, Hermann J., 39
mystery, 44, 46

New Earth, 61, 107–108
Newman, John Henry, 97
Nietzsche, Friedrich, 103–104
nihilism, 46, 68–69
"not yet in being", 79–80, 107

Omega Point, 66–68
omens, 98
Oppenheimer, Robert, 15–16
optimism, 40, 60

Pascal, Blaise, 49
Paul (Apostle), 96
Peterson, Erik, 36
petition, prayer of, 112
philosophy, 19–20, 46–47, 79–80, 99–101
Picard, Max, 91
Pieper, Josef, 80
Plato, 19, 25, 96, 99, 109
Plügge, Herbert, 27–29
Portmann, Adolph, 62–63
present, the, 50, 68
prognosis: *see* forecasting, prophecy
progress, 40, 53, 54, 56–58
prophecy, 51, 95–97, 98, 100, 103; *see also* forecasting
providence, 56

Rahner, Karl, 45, 85, 97, 101, 105, 112
Rationalism, 55
Rauschning, Hermann, 104
reason, 102
religion, 18

117

religion of reason, 55
Rensch, Bernhard, 41
resurrection, 78, 108
revolution, 83, 100
Rüstow, Alexander, 98

Scheeben, Matthias
    Joseph, 96
Schelsky, Helmut, 45
schisme profond, 68, 70
Schlier, Heinrich, 44–45
Schneider, Reinhold, 91
self-annihilation, 14–17,
    48, 91
socialism, 80
society, universal fulfill-
    ment, 93
sociology, 45
solidarity, 109–110
spes implicita, 111
Spinoza, Baruch, 20
statistics, 42, 49

status viatoris, 31, 79, 107
"strike", 69

Teilhard de Chardin,
    Pierre, 35–42, 53, 65–
    71, 84–85, 101, 106
theology, 44–47, 96
Thomas Aquinas, 77–78,
    80, 98, 105, 109–110,
    112
tradition, sacred, 55, 110
truth, triumph of, 92

utopia, 77, 79

Vico, Giambattista, 90

war, 58
Weiß, Konrad, 113
Wieser, Wolfgang, 96
will, free: *see* freedom
Wolstenholme, Gordon,
    15